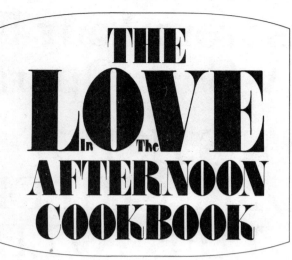

THE LOVE
In O The
AFTERNOON
COOKBOOK

Recipes from Your Favorite ABC-TV Soap Operas:

RYAN'S HOPE
ALL MY CHILDREN
ONE LIFE TO LIVE
GENERAL HOSPITAL

Recipes by Jeanne Jones
Text by Donna Swajeski

M. EVANS and COMPANY, Inc.   New York

THE LOVE
In The
AFTERNOON
COOKBOOK

To Mildred Mead—with deep appreciation for your help and talent

Love in the Afternoon, General Hospital, All My Children, One Life to Live, and *Ryan's Hope,* are trademarks of American Broadcasting Companies, Inc., licensed to M. Evans and Co., Inc.

Photographs: Marg Helgenberger (Siobhan Ryan, "Ryan's Hope"); Ilene Kristen (Delia Coleridge, "Ryan's Hope"); Susan Lucci, (Erica Kane, "All My Children"); Robin Strasser (Dorian Lord Callison, "One Life to Live"); Philip Carey (Asa Buchanan, "One Life to Live"); Denise Alexender (Lesley Webber, "General Hospital"); Jacklyn Zeman (Bobbie Spencer, "General Hospital")

Thanks are due to the following for permission to adapt recipes:

101 Productions:
   The Calculating Cook by Jeanne Jones. Copyright © 1972 by Jeanne Jones
   Diet for a Happy Heart by Jeanne Jones. Copyright © 1977 by Jeanne Jones
   More Calculating Cooking by Jeanne Jones. Copyright © 1981 by Jeanne Jones

Charles Scribner's Sons:
   The Food Lover's Diet by Jeanne Jones. Copyright © 1982 by Jeanne Jones

M. Evans and Company, Inc.:
   Stuffed Spuds by Jeanne Jones. Copyright © 1982 by Jeanne Jones

Library of Congress Cataloging in Publication Data

Jones, Jeanne.
   The love in the afternoon cookbook.

   Includes index.
   1. Cookery. 2. Soap operas—United States.
I. Swajeski, Donna.   II. Title.
TX652.J67 1983   641.5   83-5685

ISBN 0-87131-426-6 CLOTHBOUND

ISBN 0-87131-405-3 PAPERBOUND

M. Evans and Company, Inc.
216 East 49 Street
New York, New York 10017

DESIGN BY RON SHEY

Manufactured in the United States of America

9 8 7 6 5 4 3 2

Contents

Introduction

Erica Kane's Oysters Sensuelle . . . Bo Buchanan's Macho Nachos . . .
Maeve Ryan's Erin Go Broccoli Casserole . . . These are just a few of the tantalizing recipes you'll enjoy in this special cookbook that combines feasting
with fantasy. Millions of viewers tune in to ABC Daytime every day to
watch the top-rated shows "Ryan's Hope," "All My Children," "One Life to
Live," and "General Hospital." The dynamic characters from these popular
soaps have achieved a life of their own, from the exotic secret agent Robert
Scorpio to the glamorous, conniving Erica Kane. On the following pages
you'll steal a glimpse into the opulent dining rooms and cozy kitchens of
these legendary characters. Whether or not you've ever watched our soaps,
you'll be impressed by the variety of meals served with flair by the entrepre-
neurs, socialites, fashion models, and cowboys of ABC Daytime. You'll discover a bounty of recipes to win friends, steal hearts, and add a spark to dinner time.

We teamed the incomparable recipes of acclaimed food writer Jeanne
Jones with the vital and intriguing personalities that have made ABC Soaps a
household word. She is the author of eight cookbooks, including the recent
Stuffed Spuds and *The Food Lover's Diet*, and is a leading lecturer in the diet
field. Jeanne Jones also serves as a consultant on recipe and menu planning
for restaurants, health organizations, and food manufacturers. We matched
enticing recipes from her kitchen with the distinct style and character of each
soap opera hero and heroine to create dishes with star quality, just like those
served at the penthouses, pool parties, boardrooms and chic restaurants of
ABC Daytime. So whether you'd like to whip up desserts from the Crystal
Palace of Ryan's Hope or make one of Myrtle Fargate's good, old-fashioned
soups, indulge all of your cooking fantasies with *The Love in the Afternoon
Cookbook*.

Donna Marie Swajeski

RYAN'S HOPE

Siobhan Ryan

Cooking at our house is a real family affair. Everyone gets into the act and the result is a Ryan family production of delectable meals that rivals a Broadway show. As kids, Patrick and I found Mom's kitchen to be a wonderland of spicy aromas; if we were lucky we found a spoon to lick when Mom made her famous Maeve's Christmas Munchies. In fact, it never felt quite like the holidays until Mom got out her cookie cutters and we all designed stars and Christmas-tree-shaped cookies, sprinkled with red and green sugar. I have many such happy memories of meals in the Ryans' kitchen that I'd like to share with you.

I learned the following recipes at the elbow of the incomparable culinary whiz Maeve Colleary Ryan and you don't have to be Irish to enjoy them. For instance, I've developed my own special brand of Irish Soda Bread right here in New York City at Ryan's Bar. That's why I call it Manhattan Soda Bread. To me it's just like the Empire State Building—there's nothing else like it in the world.

For a different taste, I brush my Manhattan Soda Bread with Parsley Butter that adds a touch of the Irish green to the loaf. Simply take a cup of butter, soften it at room temperature and blend in ½ cup of finely chopped parsley. You can also add a tablespoon or two of green onion tops if you'd like. Soda bread is economical because it's so versatile. You can serve it plain with fresh jam or as the perfect breakfast treat with sausage and eggs. It adds punch to a sandwich too. I love to make it up in small loaves and wrap it in green tissue and ribbons for the perfect St. Patrick's Day present.

Soda Bread is also a terrific complement to my Colleary Colcannon, a classic meal of cabbage and potatoes with a twist. The special ingredient: caraway seeds, for a terrific new taste. (Did you know that caraway is an ar-

11

omatic herb of the carrot family?) I serve my Colcannon with a simmering hot and creamy broccoli casserole.

I have to admit I was one of those kids who had to be bribed to eat my vegetables. So Mom made vegetables fun with her Erin Go Broccoli Casserole, and I learned early to appreciate its fresh taste and tangy flavor. I follow my Colleary Colcannon and Erin Go Broccoli Casserole with a light Park Avenue Pudding filled with fresh bananas and oranges. When I bring this meal to the table, you can bet all Irish eyes are smiling.

Da's specialty is Top of the Mornin' Eggs. These are a fabulous brunch surprise; they're almost a tradition at Ryan's Bar. They're similar to Eggs Benedict, but instead of using muffins Top of the Mornin' Eggs are served over piping-hot baked potatoes. Especially great on cold winter mornings. Da makes his Rich Hollandaise Sauce to spoon over the eggs. But I've also included his Shortcut Hollandaise Sauce recipe, which takes only 2 minutes to prepare. This is perfect for an active family like ours; we all have to eat breakfast in a hurry and get to work.

As you might guess, I've learned to appreciate the versatility of the common potato—such an unassuming, taken-for-granted vegetable, but so high in potassium and iron. And it's chock full of B and C vitamins. Potatoes are a terrific meal in themselves because they're high in fiber so they're filling but low in calories; that makes them nonfattening. Serve potatoes whole with delicious toppings of cheese, mint or sour cream and garnish with paprika. Or make a delicious side dish out of the skins. Baked potato skins covered with melted grated Cheddar cheese are out of this world. You'll also love my brother's favorite, Patrick's Potato Soup flavored with onions and bacon. I make up a big pot of it and serve it family style. And my Potato Power Chowder with its tempting taste of celery and corn is a delicious warm-up to any meal. Or try my Pot o' Gold Potato Rolls for a new lightly sweet taste treat to liven up your bread basket. The next time you decide to serve a plain old baked potato, think of all the possibilities and try one of my various potato recipes for satisfaction guaranteed.

I've included a few casserole dishes, too, that are a must for the busy working woman. With them, I can work all day at the Police Academy and still come home to a substantial meal. For those of you who like a slightly spicier flavor to your meat and chicken, try my Green Pepper Jam. It can be used as a condiment for your dinner or as an extraordinary hors d'oeuvre served over cream cheese with crackers.

What Irish kitchen would be complete without a recipe for Irish stew? Our recipe calls for a touch of Irish whiskey to give it a saucy flavor. There's a story behind this unusual ingredient in Ryan's Irish Stew. It seems that long ago our distant Aunt Maggie, whose husband was a wee bit too fond of Irish whiskey, took to pouring it into the stew to keep it out of his reach. Whiskey loses its alcoholic content when cooked, but it adds an incomparable flavor. Try it for yourself. This recipe is so popular at Ryan's

Bar people come from miles around to taste it. And they always come back for more.

Closing time, when Ryan's Bar is quiet and we all sit around talking with friends, is dessert time. I've always had a weakness for strawberries, maybe because I'm the only redhead in the family. So I've created Siobhan's Strawberry Pie. The recipe is simple to make, but guests will swear you've slaved hours to come up with such a creamy, rich pie. I sometimes freeze a tray of mashed ripe strawberries so I'm prepared to make my tasty pie any time at all. (I also love to put a few of those frozen strawberry cubes into my ice tea for a real strawberry sensation.) You can also use frozen strawberries, pineapple and bananas to create my Irish Rose Salad. A great snack or light lunch pleaser, served on curls of fresh green lettuce.

Now Ireland has the Blarney Stone but here in New York City we have Broadway. So I created Broadway Star Cookies, a dessert that lets you really leave your mark. Before the cookies have finished baking, you take them out of the oven and make a small indentation in the dough with your thumb. Then fill this space with candied fruit, a dot of your favorite jam or a chocolate chip, and bake until done. Since it's fun for kids to participate in this recipe, Ryan and I especially love to make these cookies on rainy Saturday afternoons. Great for children's birthday parties too.

I've included some fantastic cookie and cake recipes in my collection, but dessert is never the last course in our house. At the end of dinner, Da disappears into the kitchen and returns with a tray of Irish coffee topped with fresh whipped cream. He always uses freshly ground Colombian decaffeinated coffee because it has a rich flavor but won't keep you up all night. We think Da's Irish Coffee is the perfect way to toast all those special occasions a family shares.

I guess that's why the kitchen is my favorite room in the house. It's really the heart of the Ryan family. We've celebrated anniversaries and birthdays and shared lots of laughter around our big old kitchen table. These recipes have been a special part of all our happy times. I'm sure they'll soon be a treasured part of your family's traditions too. Bring a touch of Ireland to your kitchen and enjoy these meals with all our love.

The Ryan Family Recipes

PATRICK'S POTATO SOUP
POTATO AND BACON SOUP

3 pounds potatoes, peeled
2 onions, finely chopped
¼ cup butter or corn-oil margarine
1 pound bacon
2 quarts milk
½ cup finely chopped fresh parsley
1 teaspoon orégano, crushed, using a mortar and pestle
1 teaspoon salt
½ teaspoon freshly ground black pepper
1 tablespoon Worcestershire sauce

1. Boil the potatoes and mash about two thirds of them. Cube the remaining potatoes.
2. Sauté the onions in the butter or margarine. Fry the bacon and drain. Crumble the bacon and add to the potatoes.
3. Add the milk, herbs, seasonings and sautéed onions and bring to a boil. Reduce the heat and simmer the entire mixture for about 30 minutes.

8 PORTIONS

POTATO POWER CHOWDER
CORN-POTATO CHOWDER

2 medium-size potatoes, diced
1 medium-size onion, sliced thin and separated into rings
½ cup chopped celery
1 teaspoon salt
½ cup water
2 cups cooked or canned whole-kernel corn
1½ cups milk
¼ teaspoon dried marjoram, crushed, using a mortar and pestle
Pinch of pepper
5 slices of bacon, cooked crisp and crumbled

1. Combine the potatoes, onion, celery, salt and water in a saucepan. Cover and cook for about 15 minutes, or until vegetables are tender.
2. Stir in the corn, milk, marjoram and pepper and mix thoroughly.
3. Top each serving with crumbled bacon.

4 PORTIONS

RYAN'S IRISH STEW
IRISH STEW

2 pounds lean lamb, cut into 1-inch cubes
1 large onion, coarsely chopped
2 pounds potatoes, peeled and quartered
2 large carrots, scraped and cut into ½-inch
    rounds
¼ cup finely chopped fresh parsley
¾ teaspoon salt
¼ teaspoon freshly ground black pepper
1 bay leaf
2 cups water
½ cup Irish whiskey (optional)

1. Since classically the meat in Irish stew is not browned, combine all ingredients in a soup kettle or large pan with a lid. (Or put it in a crockpot, reducing the water to 1 cup, and let it simmer all day.) Simmer, covered, for 2½ to 3 hours, or until the meat is completely tender.
2. Remove the bay leaf before serving.
4 TO 6 PORTIONS

MAEVE'S CORNED BEEF AND CABBAGE
CORNED BEEF AND CABBAGE

4 pounds lean corned beef
2 garlic cloves, cut into halves
1 cup chopped onion
2 bay leaves
10 peppercorns
2 tablespoons pickling spices
3 potatoes, peeled and quartered
6 small carrots, halved
4 celery ribs, cut into 1-inch pieces
1 head of cabbage, quartered

1. Put the corned beef in a big kettle and cover it with cold water.
2. Add the next 5 ingredients and bring to a boil. Reduce the heat and simmer for 3½ hours. You may stop at this point if you wish and refrigerate the meat until you are ready to finish the following day.
3. Remove excess fat which may have accumulated on the surface and bring liquid to a slow boil. Add the potatoes, carrots and celery. Cook for 30 minutes, or until the vegetables are tender. Remove the bay leaves. During the last 15 minutes of cooking time add the cabbage. Do not overcook the cabbage.
6 TO 8 PORTIONS

RIVERSIDE CASSOULET
CASSOULET

1 pound dried white beans (pea beans or small
    lima beans)
1 bay leaf
1 celery rib
3 parsley sprigs
1 pound pork sausage
1 large onion, chopped
2 cups chopped leftover cooked ham, turkey or
    pork chops
1 cup white wine
½ cup tomato sauce
1 cup dried bread crumbs
½ cup melted butter
1 garlic clove, minced
½ cup minced fresh parsley

1. Soak the beans, in water to cover, overnight.
2. Tie the bay leaf, celery and parsley together to form an herb bouquet. In the morning, cook the beans, in fresh water, over medium heat with the bouquet for 15 minutes. Remove the bouquet and drain the beans.
3. Brown the sausage in a skillet. Remove the sausage and sauté the onion in the fat. Com-

bine the sausage and onion with the beans and mix well. Place one third of the mixture in a large casserole.

4. Add a layer of chopped meat over the sausage and bean mixture, then another layer of beans, another layer of chopped meat and beans on the top.
5. Combine the wine and tomato sauce and pour over the casserole.
6. Combine the bread crumbs, melted butter and garlic and spread over the casserole. Sprinkle parsley over the top. Bake uncovered in a 350°F. oven for 1½ to 2 hours, or until the beans are tender.

6 TO 8 PORTIONS

ERIN GO BROCCOLI CASSEROLE

BROCCOLI AND CHEESE CASSEROLE

¼ cup chopped onion
4 tablespoons butter or corn-oil margarine
2 tablespoons flour
½ cup water
1 jar (8 ounces) pimiento cheese
2 packages (10 ounces each) frozen chopped broccoli, thawed
2 eggs, well beaten
3 tablespoons melted butter or corn-oil margarine
½ cup cracker crumbs

1. Preheat oven to 350°F. Sauté the onion in the butter. Add the flour and stir in. Add the water and stir until blended.
2. Add the pimiento cheese and mix thoroughly. Add the broccoli and eggs and again mix thoroughly.
3. Pour into an oiled 6-cup casserole. Combine the melted butter and cracker crumbs and spread over the casserole. Bake for 45 minutes.

6 PORTIONS

COLLEARY COLCANNON

COLCANNON

4 baking potatoes
4 cups finely shredded green cabbage (½ head)
3 tablespoons corn-oil margarine
½ cup lukewarm milk
4 medium-size green onions, including 2 inches of the tops, finely chopped
½ teaspoon salt
½ teaspoon caraway seeds
Freshly ground black pepper
¼ cup finely chopped fresh parsley

1. Wash the potatoes thoroughly, and dry. Pierce with the tines of a fork. Bake in a 400°F. oven for 1 hour. Remove from the oven and cool slightly.
2. While the potatoes are cooling, put the shredded cabbage in a pan with enough water to cover. Bring to a boil and boil rapidly, uncovered, for 8 minutes. Drain thoroughly, using a colander, and set aside.
3. When the potatoes are cool enough to handle, split them down the center and carefully remove the potato from the skins, being careful not to tear the skins. Set the skins aside to refill with the colcannon mixture.
4. Combine the potato pulp with the margarine and mash thoroughly, using a fork. Adding the milk a little at a time, beat the potatoes with an electric mixer. Add more milk, if necessary, to blend to a creamy consistency.
5. Add the cooked, drained cabbage to the potato mixture. Add the chopped green onions, salt, caraway seeds and pepper to taste, and mix thoroughly.
6. Refill the potato skins with the colcannon mixture. Garnish each potato with fresh parsley; if making ahead of time and reheating, add the parsley just before serving.

8 TO 12 PORTIONS

PLAZA POTATO CASSEROLE
POTATO AND CHEESE CASSEROLE

¼ cup corn-oil margarine
1 can (10¾ ounces) condensed cream of chicken
    soup, undiluted
1½ cups grated Cheddar cheese
½ cup sour cream
¼ cup snipped chives or green onion tops
6 large potatoes, cooked and mashed
Salt and pepper

1. Melt the margarine in a pan and add the chicken soup, stirring constantly.
2. Add the cheese and stir until it is melted. Stir in the sour cream and chives or green onion tops. Add the potatoes and mix thoroughly. Season to taste.
3. Pour into a lightly buttered 8-cup casserole and bake at 350°F. for 30 to 40 minutes, or until really bubbly.
6 TO 8 PORTIONS

CENTRAL PARK POTATOES
POTATOES AND ONIONS AU GRATIN

2½ to 3 pounds potatoes, unpeeled, washed
1 pound small white onions, peeled
¼ cup butter or corn-oil margarine
¼ cup flour
1½ cups milk
1½ cups light cream
½ cup chicken broth
½ pound sharp Cheddar cheese, grated
½ cup grated Parmesan cheese
¾ teaspoon salt

¼ teaspoon freshly ground black pepper
½ teaspoon seasoned salt
1 garlic clove, minced

1. Boil the potatoes in their jackets in water to cover for about 20 minutes. When cool enough to handle, peel and cut into ½-inch cubes. Place in a 2½-quart casserole dish.
2. Cook the onions in boiling water until tender, and drain. Combine with the potatoes in the casserole dish.
3. Melt the butter or margarine in a saucepan and add the flour, mixing thoroughly. When smooth, add the milk, cream and chicken broth and cook until thickened, stirring frequently. Add the cheeses and stir until melted. Add the remaining ingredients and mix well.
4. Pour the sauce over the potatoes and onions in the casserole and mix lightly. Bake, uncovered, at 350°F. for 45 minutes.
8 PORTIONS OR MORE

FIFTH AVENUE CASSEROLE
TUNA-MACARONI CASSEROLE

1 cup cooked shell macaroni
½ cup chopped walnuts
2 cups crushed potato chips
1 cup chopped celery
1 teaspoon lemon juice
½ teaspoon salt
1 can (10¾ ounces) condensed cream of chicken
    soup
2 cups tuna, flaked
¾ cup mayonnaise
1 can (4 ounces) water chestnuts, sliced, drained

1. Combine all ingredients in an oiled 6-cup casserole and mix well.
2. Bake at 350°F. for 1 hour.
4 TO 6 PORTIONS

EAST SIDE SKILLET SLAW
SKILLET SLAW

4 large slices of bacon
¼ cup cider vinegar
2 tablespoons sliced green onion
1 tablespoon brown sugar
1 teaspoon salt
4 cups shredded cabbage (about ½ medium-size head)
1 teaspoon caraway seeds

1. Cook the bacon in a skillet until crisp. Remove, drain, saving the drippings, and crumble the bacon. Set aside. Measure ¼ cup of the bacon drippings and return to the skillet.
2. Add the vinegar, green onion, brown sugar and salt to the skillet and heat through.
3. Add the cabbage and caraway seeds to the skillet and toss lightly. Top each serving with some crumbled bacon.

4 TO 6 PORTIONS

IRISH ROSE SALAD
STRAWBERRY AND PINEAPPLE SALAD

1 large package (6 ounces) strawberry Jell-O
2 cups hot water
1 can (14 ounces) crushed pineapple, drained
8 ounces frozen strawberries, thawed
2 bananas, mashed
Pinch of salt
1 cup sour cream
Lettuce for serving plates

1. Dissolve the Jell-O in the hot water and chill slightly. Add the pineapple, strawberries, bananas and pinch of salt and mix thoroughly.
2. Pour half of the mixture into a baking dish or other pan (9 x 12 inches) and chill until firm.

Do not refrigerate the remaining half.
3. After the first half has jelled, spread the sour cream evenly over the surface. Pour the remaining Jell-O mixture over the sour-cream surface and chill. Cut into 8 servings and place on chilled lettuce-lined plates.

8 PORTIONS

FRANK'S POT O' GOLD POTATO ROLLS
LIGHT POTATO ROLLS

2 envelopes of dry yeast (check the date)
¼ cup warm water
2 tablespoons sugar
2 tablespoons flour
2 medium-size potatoes, peeled and boiled
Water from cooking potatoes
⅔ cup sugar
⅔ cup corn-oil margarine
2 eggs
4 to 5 cups flour

1. Crumble the yeast into the warm water and add the 2 tablespoons sugar. Stir well. Add 2 tablespoons of flour gradually, forming a pasty mixture. Let rise in a warm place.
2. Reserve the water from cooking the potatoes (this should be about 1¼ cups). Place the drained potatoes into a blender container and add enough of the potato water to blend into a smooth mixture. Set aside.
3. Cream the ⅔ cup sugar and margarine. Add the eggs and mix well. Add the potatoes and stir well. Add the yeast mixture.
4. Gradually add the flour and knead the dough until flour is mixed in. Let dough rise until doubled in bulk.
5. Roll out and form into about 4 dozen small rolls. Place in baking pans and let rise again for about 2 hours.
6. Bake at 350°F. for 20 to 25 minutes, or until nicely browned.

4 DOZEN ROLLS

MANHATTAN SODA BREAD

IRISH SODA BREAD

2 cups all-purpose flour
1½ teaspoons baking powder
½ teaspoon baking soda
4 teaspoons pure crystalline fructose, or
    2 tablespoons sugar
½ teaspoon salt
¼ cup corn-oil margarine, chilled
⅔ cup buttermilk
1 egg, lightly beaten
2 teaspoons caraway seeds
Milk for glazing

1. Preheat oven to 325°F. Combine the flour, baking powder, baking soda, fructose or sugar, and salt in a large mixing bowl; mix well.
2. Add the margarine and, using a pastry blender, blend the mixture until it has the consistency of coarse cornmeal; set aside.
3. Combine the buttermilk and beaten egg and mix thoroughly. Add the liquid ingredients to the dry ingredients and mix well. Mix in the caraway seeds.
4. Remove the dough to a floured board and knead for 2 or 3 minutes, or until smooth and elastic. Place the dough in an oiled and floured 9-inch round cake pan and press it down so that the dough fills the entire pan. Cut a deep crease in the top of the bread so the sides will not crack while the bread is baking. Brush the top lightly with milk.
5. Bake in the preheated oven for 35 to 40 minutes, or until the top of the loaf is a light golden brown. Remove from the oven and let cool for 5 minutes, then turn out of the pan, place on a rack, and cool to room temperature. The loaf is much easier to slice when

cool. If you wish to serve the bread hot, slice, butter it if desired, wrap it in foil, and reheat in the oven.
1 ROUND LOAF

TOP OF THE MORNIN' EGGS

IRISH EGGS

2 baked potatoes
4 tablespoons butter or corn-oil margarine
½ teaspoon salt
4 slices of Canadian bacon, cooked
4 eggs, poached
¾ cup hollandaise sauce, warm (recipe follows)
Truffle or ripe olive slices for garnish

1. This recipe requires that several items be cooking at once, so organize your time accordingly.
2. Cut the potatoes into halves. With a knife slit the edges of the potato shells at 1-inch intervals, and flatten the shells and pulp to form the 4 bases (the "muffins") for the other ingredients. Work 1 tablespoon of butter and ⅛ teaspoon of salt into each potato half. Keep warm.
3. Place 1 slice of Canadian bacon on each potato half, top with a poached egg, and then with some warm hollandaise sauce.
4. Garnish with slices of truffle or ripe olive.
4 PORTIONS

RICH HOLLANDAISE SAUCE

2 egg yolks
¼ teaspoon salt
Pinch of cayenne pepper

½ cup melted butter or corn-oil margarine
1 tablespoon freshly squeezed lemon juice

1. Beat the egg yolks, using a wire whisk or an eggbeater, until thick and very yellow. Add the salt and cayenne. Start adding the melted butter or margarine slowly, about 1 teaspoon at a time, beating constantly, until you have added at least half of it.
2. Add the lemon juice to the remaining butter or margarine and mix well. Continue adding butter slowly to the egg yolks, beating constantly, until the sauce is thick.
ABOUT ½ CUP

SHORTCUT HOLLANDAISE SAUCE
MOCK HOLLANDAISE

(when you're in a hurry)

1 cup mayonnaise
2 tablespoons butter or corn-oil margarine
2 tablespoons freshly squeezed lemon juice
⅛ teaspoon salt

1. Warm the mayonnaise in a double boiler over hot, but not boiling, water. Dot with the butter or margarine and stir with a whisk until it is melted.
2. Add the lemon juice and salt and mix well. Use immediately or refrigerate and reheat just before using.
ABOUT 1 CUP

GREEN PEPPER JAM

2 cups chopped green bell pepper
¼ medium-size onion
2 teaspoons freshly squeezed lemon juice
3 small or 2 medium-size chili peppers, washed and seeded

¾ cup sugar
1 cup white vinegar
1 bottle (6 ounces) Certo
3 or 4 drops of green food coloring

1. Clean and dry the bell peppers and chili peppers so there will be no water on them.
2. Place the chopped bell pepper, onion, lemon juice and chili peppers in a blender container and blend until smooth.
3. In a saucepan, combine the blended ingredients with the sugar and vinegar. Bring to a boil and cook for 5 minutes. Add the Certo and boil for an additional 2 minutes.
4. Add the green food coloring and mix well. Pour into sterilized jars and seal tightly. Serve over cream cheese with crackers or as a condiment with meat or poultry.
3 OR 4 JARS, 6-OUNCE SIZE

CANDIED DANNY BOYS
ORANGES IN SYRUP

2 large grapefruits, peeled
2 large navel oranges, peeled
½ cup water
1 cup sugar or ⅔ cup pure crystalline fructose
2 tablespoons finely chopped orange rind
½ cup canned kumquats, seeded and thinly sliced

1. Cut the grapefruits and oranges into pieces over a bowl to retain all the juice; remove all membranes.
2. Place the water and sugar in a saucepan. Add the orange rind and cook over medium heat for 6 to 8 minutes without stirring
3. Pour the hot mixture over the orange and grapefruit pieces in the bowl and allow to come to room temperature. Add the kumquats and mix well. Store in the refrigerator. This will keep for several days.
6 OR MORE PORTIONS

SIOBHAN'S STRAWBERRY PIE
STRAWBERRY PIE

Pastry for 1-crust 9-inch pie
1 quart fresh strawberries, washed and hulled
¼ cup water
1 cup sugar or ⅔ cup pure crystalline fructose
3 tablespoons cornstarch
1 tablespoon freshly squeezed lemon juice
½ cup whipping cream

1. Prepare the pastry and bake it. Set aside to cool.
2. Separate the strawberries into 2 equal portions, placing the larger berries in the baked crust and the smaller berries in a saucepan.
3. Mash the smaller strawberries and add the water, sugar and cornstarch and mix well. Bring to a boil. Reduce the heat and simmer, stirring, until thick and clear.
4. Remove from the heat, add the lemon juice and mix well. Cool slightly. Pour sauce over the strawberries in the piecrust, spreading evenly. Chill the pie in the refrigerator.
5. Just before serving, whip the cream. Place the whipped cream in a pastry bag and decorate the circumference of the pie filling.

6 TO 8 PORTIONS

EMERALD ISLE CAKE
WALNUT MINT CAKE

½ large (10-inch) angel-food cake
⅔ cup butter or corn-oil margarine
1¼ cups powdered sugar
3 eggs, separated
⅛ teaspoon peppermint flavoring
Green food coloring
½ cup chopped walnuts
8 macaroons, crushed
1 cup whipping cream
14 coarsely broken walnut halves
Fresh mint sprigs for garnish (optional)

1. Butter the inside of a 9-inch round springform pan. Break the angel-food cake into bite-size pieces and line the bottom and sides of the pan with the pieces.
2. Cream the butter or margarine and the powdered sugar until light and fluffy. Beat the egg yolks slightly and add to the creamed mixture, beating well.
3. Stir in the peppermint flavoring and enough green coloring to make the mixture pale green. Fold in the chopped walnuts and crushed macaroons.
4. Beat the egg whites until stiff and fold in. Spoon the mixture over the cake pieces in the mold. Chill overnight in the refrigerator.
5. When ready to serve, unmold. Whip the cream and spread over the top and sides of the cake and garnish with the broken walnut halves. Use mint sprigs for additional garnish on each serving if available.

8 PORTIONS

PARK AVENUE PUDDING
GOLDEN PUDDING

1 can (16 ounces) pineapple chunks in juice
2 oranges, peeled and diced
¼ cup freshly squeezed orange juice
2 eggs, lightly beaten
⅓ cup sugar or ¼ cup pure crystalline fructose
1 tablespoon cornstarch
2 bananas, peeled

1. Drain the pineapple chunks and reserve the juice. Combine the diced oranges with the pineapple chunks and refrigerate.
2. Combine the orange juice, reserved pineapple juice, eggs, sugar and cornstarch in a saucepan and bring to a boil. Reduce the heat and stir until thickened. Pour into a bowl and refrigerate.
3. Just before serving, slice the bananas and combine with the pineapple-orange mixture.
4. Pour the sauce over the fruit.

6 PORTIONS

BROADWAY STAR COOKIES
GOLDEN THUMBPRINT COOKIES

½ cup butter
⅓ cup firmly packed golden brown sugar
1 egg, separated
½ teaspoon vanilla extract
1 cup flour
¼ teaspoon salt
¾ cup finely chopped walnuts
Candied fruit, jam or chocolate chips

1. Cream the butter, sugar and egg yolk until light and fluffy. Add the vanilla extract and mix well. Stir in the flour and salt.
2. Roll dough into 1-inch balls. Dip into the slightly beaten egg white and roll in the chopped walnuts.
3. Place on an ungreased baking sheet and bake in a preheated 375°F. oven for 5 minutes. Remove from the oven and quickly indent each cookie with your thumb. Return to the oven and bake for 8 minutes longer.
4. Cool on a wire rack. While they are cooling, fill each thumbprint with a small piece of candied fruit, a bit of jam or a chocolate chip.

ABOUT 3 DOZEN COOKIES

MAEVE'S CHRISTMAS MUNCHIES
CHRISTMAS COOKIES

1½ cups powdered sugar
1 cup butter or corn-oil margarine
1 egg
1 teaspoon vanilla extract
½ teaspoon almond extract
2½ cups sifted flour
1 teaspoon baking soda
1 teaspoon cream of tartar
Green and red sugar for the tops

1. Combine the sugar and butter. Add the egg and the extracts and mix well.
2. Sift the dry ingredients together and stir in thoroughly. Refrigerate for 2 to 3 hours.
3. Preheat oven to 375°F. Divide the dough into halves and roll out to 3/16-inch thickness. Cut with variously shaped Christmas cookie cutters and sprinkle with green or red sugar, or with a combination of both.
4. Place on a lightly oiled baking sheet and bake for 7 to 8 minutes, or until golden brown.

ABOUT 5 DOZEN COOKIES

DA'S IRISH COFFEE
IRISH COFFEE

1 cup strong, freshly made coffee or decaffeinated coffee
1½ teaspoons sugar, or 1 teaspoon pure crystalline fructose
1½ ounces Irish whiskey
2 tablespoons whipping cream, whipped

1. Pour the coffee into the serving glass. Add the sugar or fructose and Irish whiskey, and stir well. Top with whipped cream.

1 PORTION

Delia Coleridge

Get ready for the most phenomenal desserts that ever crossed a dining room table. You're invited to the premiere of my collection of Delia's Delectable Desserts. These incomparable recipes have won me many standing ovations and put my restaurant, the Crystal Palace, on the map. Not for me the conventional cakes and cookies; I'll leave that to Sara Lee. Because I like to make entrances. I love to be center stage, in the spotlight. So I don't just make desserts (my absolute favorite part of a meal), I make dessert legends. Try my special desserts. You'll swear they're fresh from the ovens of the finest French bakeries. They're sugar and spice and everything nice. And best of all, they're easy to make.

There's nothing like the oohs and aahs you'll get with my Flaming Passion Crêpes. What a dramatic dessert you can create like magic right at the table in front of your guests! When you light the gleaming brandy in the chafing dish and stir the hot sauce over these luscious crêpes, you'll make dessert a festive occasion. My Flaming Passion Crêpes are similar to Crêpes Suzette but with a special Delia twist: the crêpes are filled with rich yummy ice cream. Don't hold back, I always say! Vary assorted flavors of ice cream for an even more unusual taste. Or mix two flavors in one crêpe for a devilish difference. And since you'll want to spend more time with your guests and less time in the kitchen, these can be prepared ahead of time. Roll the ice cream in the crêpes, put them in a covered container, and freeze them. Then, during dinner sneak away for 1 minute when everyone's beginning their entrées and take the crêpes out of the freezer to soften. The hot flaming sauce does the rest. Sometimes I garnish these crêpes or my Crystal Palace Crêpes with sliced almonds, pecans or walnuts for a crunchy taste that'll drive guests nuts! (With any leftover walnuts or almonds, you can make my renowned Almond Temptation. No one has yet been able to resist this one!)

Many a famous Broadway actor or movie star drops into my Crystal Palace restaurant for dessert. My desserts have started gossip, prompted romances, and broken hearts. People turn out in crowds to sample dessert sensations like my Raspberry Rapture. It's a terrific light dessert and can be served with fruit salad instead of the more conventional sherbet. Two of the most popular recipes on the menu are my Bavarian Cream Dream and the incomparable Oh La La Chocolat. I picked this one up from a visiting French Count and it's my version of Pots De Crème Au Chocolat, a dessert the French treasure almost as much as the Eiffel Tower. Serve it in steaming lidded *pots de crème* china for a nice touch, or simply substitute custard cups and end your meals with this Parisian delight. *Magnifique!*

I've also turned many heads with my Chocolate Mousse Paradise. This dessert is extra rich but it takes just about 2 minutes to make. But that will be our secret.

Roger's favorite is my Mischievous Meringue Cake, though he's always teasing me about it. You make this dessert ahead of time and let it sit overnight. He says this way I have all day to get into trouble. I don't know what he's talking about. I've turned over a new leaf. I put all my energies into designing new and exotic desserts like Babas au Rhum. It might take a little extra time to prepare this dish but it's worth it. You'll need baba pans, individual dariole molds or custard cups for this one. Not only is it fun to make this unusual dessert, but it's a real challenge to come up with new ways to serve it. Since I love being unpredictable, when Maeve celebrated her last birthday, I prepared Babas au Rhum in place of a plain old birthday cake. This recipe is a little more adventurous, but what a treat to bring out a silver tray filled with babas with a birthday candle in the center of each one. It's so delicious, it's almost a sin.

I look for dessert inspirations wherever I can find them. And sometimes I don't have to look any farther than my neighborhood fruit stand since I'm crazy for lemons. Whenever I have a small dinner party I always treat friends to my showstopper, Delia's De-Lemon Delight. This is a lemon dream made in a spring mold with a frame of golden ladyfingers. You can set out silver bowls filled with sauce and nuts so guests can help themselves to just the right amount of topping. A few encore helpings of this lemon sensation and you'll have even the most bashful guest puckering up with delight.

Even Little John has inspired new recipes! His favorite food is peanut butter. I tried to interest him in other things, but he's a loyal fan. So if you can't beat 'em, join 'em; you'll love Little John's Peanut Butter Soufflé with fresh roasted peanuts. It's got the fun of peanut butter with the elegance of a soufflé. And peanut butter is good for you. Peanuts are high in protein and potassium and cause no tooth decay.

What I really love best about desserts is the way they evoke wonderful childhood memories. Apple pies baking hot in the oven and brownies cooling on the kitchen window sill can bring back the most delicious thoughts of home and family. On her visits to New York, the Ryans' Aunt Annie used to make a fresh, bubbling-hot, flaky-crusted blueberry pie that really started me on my quest for the perfect desserts. A slice of tart blueberry pie crowned with a melting scoop of vanilla ice cream is the simplest way to bring a smile to anyone's face. Whenever I get a case of the blues, I pull out my blueberries and in 40 minutes I'm happily helping myself to Aunt Annie's prizewinning blueberry pie. Though I love my fancy forays into exotic dessert making, sometimes it's nice to get back to basics . . . thanks to Aunt Annie.

Since I never want anyone to forget me or my dessert delectables, I make two spectacular cookie bars for my friends they can wrap up and take with them to work or on a picnic or even to the movies. You'll love my Kooky Coconut Crunch and my Triple Trouble Bars with three scrumptious layers of coconut and graham-cracker crumbs, rich vanilla pudding and lush melted chocolate. Believe me, this is triple trouble you won't mind getting into.

After all, no matter how good the dinner, it's the dessert people walk away remembering. And the dessert maker. Desserts end the meal on a high note and bring down the curtain perfectly on the best of dinners. Men have loved me for my charm and beauty, but it's my delectable desserts that bring them back every time.

Delia's Delectable Desserts

DELIA'S DE-LEMON DELIGHT
LEMON CHARLOTTE RUSSE

26 ladyfingers
1 envelope unflavored gelatin
4 tablespoons freshly squeezed lemon juice
5 eggs
½ cup sugar
Pinch of salt
2 teaspoons grated lemon rind
1 cup heavy cream, whipped
¼ cup chopped raw almonds (optional)
GOLDEN SAUCE
3 tablespoons apricot preserves
3 tablespoons orange marmalade
2 tablespoons Grand Marnier liqueur
1 tablespoon freshly squeezed lemon juice

1. Line the inner circumference of a 10-inch springform mold with ladyfingers, standing them up like soldiers with the flat sides facing in. Set aside.
2. Dissolve the gelatin in the lemon juice and melt over hot water. Place the eggs, sugar and salt in the top pan of a 2-quart double boiler over simmering water. Beat until the eggs are thick, very light in color, and have practically filled the 2-quart saucepan.
3. Add the melted gelatin and the grated lemon rind and beat for a few seconds more. Cool a little and add the whipped cream. Fold with care (the mixture will diminish a little in volume) and pour into the ladyfinger-lined springform mold. Chill for several hours before serving.
4. Place the almonds on a pan in the center of a 350°F. oven for 8 to 10 minutes, or until golden brown. Watch them carefully as they burn easily. Set aside.
5. Make the sauce: Melt the preserves and marmalade. Add the Grand Marnier and lemon juice and mix well.
6. To serve, place the mold on a serving dish and release the outside of the mold, being careful not to dislodge the ladyfingers. Spoon the sauce over the top and sprinkle toasted almonds over each serving; or, if you prefer, serve only with more whipped cream over the top.

8 TO 12 PORTIONS

LITTLE JOHN'S PEANUT BUTTER SOUFFLÉ
PEANUT BUTTER SOUFFLÉ

½ cup unhomogenized peanut butter
½ cup honey
2 envelopes unflavored gelatin
1 cup cold water
2 egg yolks
2 teaspoons vanilla extract
8 egg whites
⅛ teaspoon cream of tartar
1 cup whipping cream
1 tablespoon dry roasted peanuts, finely chopped

1. Combine the peanut butter and honey and set aside.
2. Soften the gelatin in the cold water for 5 minutes.
3. Beat the egg yolks with a mixer or wire whisk until foamy. Beat in the softened gelatin. Pour the mixture into the top pan of a double boiler and set over hot water. Place over moderate heat. Cook, stirring constantly, until thick enough to lightly coat a metal spoon. Do not allow the mixture to come to a boil!
4. Remove the pan from the heat and stir in the peanut-butter mixture and vanilla extract. Pour the mixture into a large mixing bowl and refrigerate until thickened to a syrupy consistency, about 30 minutes.
5. Beat the egg whites and cream of tartar until they are stiff but not dry. Set aside.
6. In another bowl, beat the whipping cream until it holds soft peaks. Pour the whipped cream into the peanut-butter mixture and blend thoroughly. Then fold the beaten egg whites into the cream and peanut-butter mixture, folding until no streaks of white show.
7. Wrap a wax-paper collar around a 7½-inch (1½-quart) soufflé dish. It should rise 5 inches above the rim of the dish. Secure the collar with string or tape. Spoon the soufflé mixture into the collared dish and refrigerate for at least 4 hours before removing the collar and serving the soufflé.
8. Sprinkle the chopped peanuts lightly over the top for garnish.

12 PORTIONS

RASPBERRY RAPTURE
RASPBERRY WHIP

This is a wonderful light dessert. It is also delicious served with fruit salad as a luncheon instead of the more traditional sherbet.

1 package (3 ounces) raspberry-flavored Jell-O
½ cup sugar, or ¼ cup pure crystalline fructose
2 bananas, mashed
⅓ cup youngberry or blackberry jelly, mashed
1 cup whipping cream

1. Make the Jell-O, following the directions on the package, and refrigerate until it has a syrupy consistency.
2. Add all other ingredients except the whipping cream to the slightly chilled Jell-O and whip until thick and again syrupy in consistency. Set aside.
3. Whip the whipping cream until it will hold soft peaks. Do not overwhip.
4. Fold the whipped cream into the Jell-O mixture carefully and thoroughly.
5. Refrigerate, covered, for several hours before serving.

4 PORTIONS

BAVARIAN CREAM DREAM

BAVARIAN CREAM WITH APRICOT SAUCE

1½ teaspoons unflavored gelatin
2 tablespoons cool water
3 egg yolks, lightly beaten
⅓ cup sugar, or ¼ cup pure crystalline fructose
1 cup milk
2 teaspoons vanilla extract
1 cup whipping cream
APRICOT SAUCE
¾ cup apricot jam
¼ cup water
1 tablespoon sugar, or 2 teaspoons pure
   crystalline fructose
2 tablespoons kirsch

1. Add the gelatin to the water and allow to soften. Set aside.
2. Combine the beaten egg yolks and sugar and blend until smooth.
3. Scald the milk. Remove the pan from the heat. Add the egg-yolk and sugar mixture and mix well. Return the saucepan to the heat and cook, stirring constantly, until it comes just to the boiling point. Do not allow to boil!
4. Remove from the heat and add the vanilla extract and softened gelatin, stirring until the gelatin is completely dissolved. Continue to stir from time to time until the mixture reaches room temperature.
5. Beat the whipping cream until it holds firm peaks. Fold the whipped cream into the custard mixture and spoon into a serving dish. Cover and refrigerate until firm.
6. While the Bavarian cream is jelling, make the apricot sauce. Combine all ingredients except

the kirsch in a saucepan and slowly bring to a boil. Cook for 10 minutes, stirring frequently to avoid scorching.
7. Cool sauce slightly and then rub through a sieve. Add the kirsch and mix well. If using the same day, do not refrigerate the sauce; however, if you are making it in advance, cover and refrigerate. Remove from the refrigerator and bring to room temperature before spooning over the cold Bavarian cream.

4 TO 6 PORTIONS

CHOCOLATE MOUSSE PARADISE

QUICK AND EASY CHOCOLATE MOUSSE

2 cups semisweet chocolate chips
1½ teaspoons vanilla extract
Pinch of salt
1½ cups whipping cream, heated to the boiling
   point
6 egg yolks
2 egg whites
Whipped cream (optional)

1. Combine the chocolate chips, vanilla extract and salt in a blender container and blend for 30 seconds.
2. Add the hot cream and continue mixing for 30 seconds more, or until the chocolate is completely melted.
3. Add the egg yolks and mix for about 5 seconds. Transfer batter to a bowl and allow it to cool. Beat the egg whites until stiff peaks form. Gently fold into the chocolate mixture.
4. Place in a serving bowl or 4 to 6 sherbert glasses. Cover with plastic wrap and chill. Serve with whipped cream if desired.

4 TO 6 PORTIONS

OH LA LA CHOCOLAT
POTS DE CRÈME AU CHOCOLAT

6 eggs at room temperature
6 ounces semisweet chocolate
Whipped cream as desired

1. Separate the eggs, being careful not to get any yolk in the whites.
2. Beat the egg whites until stiff but not dry and set aside.
3. Melt the chocolate in the top of a double boiler. Stir the yolks into the chocolate, beating until the mixture is completely smooth.
4. Remove from the heat. Fold the egg whites carefully into the chocolate mixture. Do not overmix.
5. Spoon the mixture into *pots de crème* pots or custard cups. Before serving, add a dollop of whipped cream to the top of each serving.

6 TO 8 PORTIONS

FLAMING PASSION CRÊPES
CRÊPES SUZETTE WITH ICE CREAM

1 cup fresh orange juice
2 teaspoons cornstarch
3 tablespoons sugar, or 2 tablespoons pure crystalline fructose
1 tablespoon freshly grated orange rind (use only the colored part of the peel)
¼ cup orange liqueur (Grand Marnier is best)
1 tablespoon butter or corn-oil margarine
4 crêpes (recipe follows)
½ pint vanilla ice cream
2 tablespoons brandy for flaming

1. Pour the orange juice into a saucepan. Add the cornstarch and sugar to the juice, and stir until the cornstarch is dissolved.
2. Bring slowly to a boil and simmer, stirring constantly with a wire whisk, until slightly thickened. Remove the pan from the heat.
3. Add the grated orange rind, orange liqueur and butter or margarine. Stir sauce until it is completely melted. Pour sauce into a heated chafing dish.
4. Spoon ¼ cup ice cream down the center of each crêpe and fold the crêpe around the ice cream. Place the crêpes, seam side down, on a serving platter.
5. Pour the brandy into the sauce in the chafing dish. Light the sauce with a long match, stirring until the flame goes out.
6. Spoon the hot sauce over the tops of the crêpes and serve immediately.

4 PORTIONS

CRYSTAL PALACE CRÊPES
CRÊPES

1 cup milk
¾ cup all-purpose flour
¼ teaspoon salt
2 large eggs at room temperature, lightly beaten
1 tablespoon butter

1. Combine the milk, flour and salt in a bowl and beat with an egg beater until completely smooth.
2. Quickly beat in the eggs, mixing well.
3. In a heated crêpe pan or medium-size round-bottom skillet, melt the butter, tilting the pan to cover the entire inner surface. Pour the excess butter into the crêpe batter.
4. Pour in enough crêpe batter to barely cover the bottom of the pan, about 2 tablespoons. Grasping the handle of the skillet in your

hand, quickly roll the pan around so the batter will spread over the bottom. Cook the crêpe until browned on the bottom, then turn to brown the other side.

(The secret of keeping crêpes pliable: Heat a covered casserole; as crêpes are cooked, stack them in the warm casserole. To do them efficiently, you have to have everything assembled so that your system of pouring, rolling, turning and storing becomes simple!)

8 CRÊPES

Note: Crêpes can be frozen successfully. They can also be made the day before and stored in the refrigerator. If you are going to store them, separate each 2 crêpes with a slice of wax paper or aluminum foil so that they will not stick together. Store them in a sealed container or wrapped in foil. Before filling the crêpes, they must be thawed to room temperature; cold crêpes will break when rolled.

MISCHIEVOUS MERINGUE CAKE
MERINGUE CAKE

10 egg whites
¼ teaspoon salt
½ teaspoon cream of tartar
2 cups sugar
1 teaspoon vanilla extract
Butter for cake pans
1 cup whipping cream
Fresh fruit as desired

1. Preheat oven to 450°F. for at least 30 minutes.
2. Beat the egg whites with the salt and cream of tartar until they are stiff but not dry.
3. Add the sugar, a little at a time, and then the vanilla extract. Continue beating until the egg whites again hold stiff peaks.

4. Butter two 9-inch round cake pans. Spread half of the meringue into each pan and place the cake pans in the center of the preheated oven. At once turn off the oven! Allow the cakes to stand overnight, or for at least 5 hours. Do not open the oven door!
5. To serve, put whipped cream between the layers of the cake and on the top add a fresh fruit such as raspberries, strawberries or peaches as desired.

6 PORTIONS

PUFF OF LEMON CAKE
LEMON JELL-O CAKE

1 package (18½ ounces) yellow cake mix
1 package (3 ounces) lemon-flavored Jell-O
¾ cup corn oil
¾ cup apricot nectar
4 eggs
2 teaspoons lemon extract
GLAZE
1 tablespoon butter
½ cup powdered sugar
Dash of cream
Grated rind of 1 lemon
Lemon juice as needed

1. Combine the cake mix and the Jell-O. Add the oil and apricot nectar.
2. Separate the eggs. Add the yolks to the mixture and mix well. Beat the egg whites until they are stiff but not dry and fold into the mixture. Add the lemon extract and mix lightly.
3. Pour into an oiled 2-quart baking dish and bake at 325°F. for 30 to 35 minutes, or until done. Cool before glazing.
4. Combine all glaze ingredients, using as much lemon juice as is needed for the desired consistency and flavor; mix well. Spread over the top of the cake.

8 PORTIONS

NUTS FOR FRUITCAKES
RICH WALNUT FRUITCAKE

2 cups coarsely chopped walnuts
2 teaspoons butter
2 cups seedless raisins
1 cup golden raisins
1 cup chopped pitted dates
1 pound diced mixed preserved fruits
2½ cups sifted flour
1 cup sugar
1½ teaspoons double-acting baking powder
1 teaspoon salt
1 cup shortening
½ cup honey
½ cup orange juice
1 tablespoon lemon juice
4 eggs

1. Preheat oven to 350°F. Spread the chopped walnuts on a cookie sheet and dot with butter. Rinse the raisins in cold water and place in a covered casserole. Place both the cookie sheet and the casserole in the oven. Remove the walnuts after 15 minutes and set aside. Continue to bake the raisins for another 10 to 15 minutes. Remove from the oven and set aside.
2. Reduce oven heat to 250°F. Grease two loaf pans, each 9 x 5 x 3 inches, and line with 2 layers of wax paper, greasing both layers generously.
3. In a bowl, combine the toasted walnuts, raisins, dates and preserved fruits and sift 1 cup of flour over the mixture; mix well.
4. Into a large bowl sift remaining 1½ cups of flour with the sugar, baking powder and salt. Add the shortening, honey and fruit juices and beat with an electric mixer at low to me-dium speed, scraping the bowl and beaters as necessary.
5. Add the eggs, one at a time, beating thoroughly after each addition. Beat one minute more.
6. Pour the batter over the floured nut mixture and stir until well mixed. Spoon into the loaf pans. Place a small shallow pan of water on the floor of the oven. Bake the fruitcakes until no imprint remains when a cake top is touched by the fingertips. Cool completely in the pans on a wire rack. Remove from the pans and peel off the paper.

2 LOAVES

BABAS AU RHUM

Babas au Rhum are said to have been invented by Stanislas Leszczyński, the exiled King of Poland, when he sprinkled his dry Kugelhopf with rum. It was so good he named it after his favorite character, Ali Baba.

BABAS
1 package active dry yeast (check the date before using)
3 tablespoons lukewarm water
1¾ cups all-purpose flour, sifted
1 tablespoon sugar, or 2 teaspoons pure crystalline fructose
1 teaspoon salt
4 eggs, beaten
½ cup dried currants or raisins
¼ cup dark rum
¼ cup water
½ cup corn-oil margarine, at room temperature
SYRUP
1 cup corn syrup or liquid fructose
2 cups water
Rind of 1 lemon, yellow only, cut into strips

Juice of 1 lemon (¼ cup freshly squeezed lemon juice)
½ cup dark rum
1 cup whipping cream, whipped

1. Combine the dry yeast and lukewarm water and allow to stand for 5 minutes.
2. Sift the flour into a large warm mixing bowl. Make a well in the center of the flour, pour in the yeast mixture, and mix well, using a large spoon.
3. Add the sugar or fructose and again mix well. Add the salt and the beaten eggs.
4. Beat until the dough is smooth, with the spoon raising the dough and letting it fall back into the bowl, making a slapping sound, for at least 5 minutes, or until the dough becomes smooth and elastic.
5. Cover the bowl with a damp cloth and allow to stand in a warm place for 1 hour, or until the dough doubles in bulk. While the dough is rising, soak the currants in ¼ cup rum combined with ¼ cup water.
6. When the dough has risen, add the margarine to the dough and beat until smooth. Drain the liquid from the currants and add the currants to the dough.
7. Drop the dough from a spoon into 10 baba pans, individual dariole molds or custard cups which have been sprayed with a nonstick spray. If you are using individual dariole molds or custard cups, place them on a baking sheet before filling them. Fill the molds half full. Cover them with a damp cloth and allow to rise in a warm place for 1 hour, or until the molds are almost full. Check to be sure the dough is not sticking to the cloth.
8. When the dough has risen to the top of the molds, bake the babas in a preheated 400°F. oven for 20 minutes, or until they begin to shrink from the sides of the molds. When possible, make the babas the day before you plan to serve them because the drier the baba, the more syrup it will absorb, and therefore the more luscious it will be.
9. To make the syrup, combine the corn syrup or liquid fructose, water, lemon rind and lemon juice in a large saucepan. Slowly bring the syrup to a boil, reduce the heat, and simmer for 5 minutes.
10. Remove the syrup from the heat and place the babas a few at a time into the very hot syrup, turning them over several times to make sure they have absorbed as much syrup as possible. The babas will swell and be very shiny.
11. Using a large slotted spoon, remove babas from the syrup and place them on a rack to cool. Just before serving, sprinkle the rum evenly over the babas. Spoon a dollop of whipped cream over each baba before serving.
12. Wrap the babas you are not going to use tightly in foil and freeze them for future use.

10 PORTIONS

FUDGE FANTASY
CHOCOLATE FUDGE ICING

1 cup less 1 tablespoon of white sugar
½ cup plus 1 tablespoon of butter
⅓ cup heavy cream
1 package (12 ounces) chocolate chips
1 tablespoon vanilla extract

1. Place the sugar, butter and cream in a pan and bring to a boil. Stir till butter melts.
2. Remove from the heat, add the chocolate chips, and stir vigorously. Add the vanilla extract and mix well. Spread on cake or cookies.

ENOUGH FOR 9-INCH CAKE OR 2 DOZEN COOKIES

Variation: *Hot Fudge Sundae:* Serve the icing hot over vanilla ice cream.

AUNT ANNIE'S BLUEBERRY PIE
BLUEBERRY PIE

PIECRUST
2 cups flour
¼ teaspoon salt
¾ cup shortening
1 tablespoon lemon juice
3 to 4 tablespoons cold water
FILLING
1 can (24 ounces) blueberries
1 cup sugar
2 tablespoons cornstarch
1 tablespoon freshly squeezed lemon juice

1. Make the piecrust: Combine the flour and salt. Add the shortening, lemon juice and as much cold water as needed to make pastry stick together; blend with a pastry blender. Press into the bottom and sides of a 9-inch pie pan, smoothing the edges. Set aside.
2. Combine all filling ingredients, using salt to taste, in a saucepan and cook over medium heat until thickened, stirring frequently.
3. Pour filling into the unbaked piecrust and bake at 350°F. for 35 to 40 minutes.

6 PORTIONS

OPULENT BROWNIES
BROWNIES WITH MACADAMIA NUTS

2 cups sugar
4 ounces Baker's unsweetened chocolate
½ cup butter or corn-oil margarine
4 eggs, lightly beaten
¼ teaspoon salt
1 teaspoon vanilla extract
1 cup all-purpose flour, sifted
1 cup coarsely chopped macadamia nuts

1. Place the chocolate and butter or margarine in a saucepan over low heat and melt, mixing well. Remove from the heat and cool.
2. Beat the eggs and add the salt. Add the sugar gradually, continuing to beat until light and creamy.
3. Fold in the chocolate mixture and the vanilla extract. Add the flour gradually and beat until the batter is smooth. Fold in the cup of nut meats.
4. Line a baking pan 9 x 13 inches with heavy wax paper, or use a nonstick pan. Pour the batter into the pan and bake at 325°F. for 30 minutes. Cool and cut into rectangles.

24 BROWNIES

TRIPLE TROUBLE BARS
WALNUT CHOCOLATE BARS

LAYER 1
½ cup butter
4 tablespoons cocoa powder
½ cup powdered sugar
1 egg, lightly beaten
1 teaspoon vanilla extract
½ cup chopped walnuts
2 cups graham-cracker crumbs
1 cup grated coconut, packed firmly
LAYER 2
¼ cup butter
3 tablespoons heavy cream
1 teaspoon vanilla extract
2 teaspoons dry vanilla pudding mix
2 cups powdered sugar
LAYER 3
1 chocolate bar, 9¾ ounces

1. Layer 1: Melt the butter and cocoa in the top pan of a double boiler over hot water. Add the powdered sugar, egg and vanilla extract. Combine the nuts, crumbs and coconut. Add to the butter and cocoa. Mix well and press into a baking pan 9 x 13 inches. Chill.
2. Layer 2: Melt the butter, cream and vanilla extract. Add the pudding and cook for 1 minute, stirring constantly. Remove from the heat and add the powdered sugar. Blend well and spread over the first layer. Chill.

3. Layer 3: Melt the chocolate bar and spread over the second layer. Refrigerate. Bring to room temperature before attempting to cut or the chocolate will crumble after refrigeration.
12 TO 18 BARS

KOOKY COCONUT CRUNCH
COCONUT WALNUT COOKIE BARS

¼ cup soft butter or corn-oil margarine
½ cup firmly packed brown sugar
1 cup sifted flour
2 eggs, unbeaten
1 cup brown sugar
1 teaspoon vanilla extract
¼ teaspoon salt
1 cup cornflakes
1 cup shredded coconut
1 cup chopped walnuts

1. Preheat oven to 350°F. Combine the butter, sugar and flour and mix well with an electric mixer. Press into an oiled baking pan 8 x 12 inches. Bake for 15 minutes. Remove from the oven.
2. Combine the eggs and brown sugar and beat until light and fluffy. Beat in the rest of the ingredients at low speed until just mixed. Spread over the baked layer. Bake for another 20 minutes.
3. Cut into bars while warm.
3½ DOZEN SMALL BARS

NUTCRACKER SWEETS
SPICED NUTS

⅓ cup sugar, or ¼ cup pure crystalline fructose
½ cup cornstarch
2 teaspoons ground cinnamon
½ teaspoon ground allspice
¼ teaspoon ground nutmeg
⅛ teaspoon ground ginger
1 egg white, lightly beaten
1 cup walnut halves (¼ pound)
1 cup whole almonds (¼ pound)

1. Preheat oven to 250°F. Put the sugar or fructose, cornstarch, cinnamon, allspice, nutmeg and ginger into a bowl. Mix well and set aside.
2. Beat the egg white in a bowl. Add the nuts and mix well. Coat each nut with the sugar-spice mixture. Shake excess dry mixture from each nut and place nuts on a well-oiled or nonstick cookie sheet. Be sure the nuts are well separated on the cookie sheet.
3. Bake in the 250°F. oven for 1½ hours. Remove from the cookie sheet and store in a tightly covered container.

2 CUPS SPICED NUTS

ALMOND TEMPTATION
CHOCOLATE NUT CANDY

2 cups sugar
3 tablespoons water
1 pound pure butter
2 cups slivered almonds
½ pound milk chocolate bar
1 cup coarsely chopped walnuts

1. Butter a baking pan 9 x 13 inches and set aside. Combine the sugar, water and butter in a pan and bring to a boil over low or medium heat (250°F. on a candy thermometer).
2. Add the slivered almonds and boil to 300°F., stirring constantly with a wooden spoon so the mixture won't burn.
3. Pour the mixture into the pan and spread to the edges with a rubber spatula. Let cool.
4. Melt the chocolate bar in the top pan of a double boiler over hot water and spread over the candy mixture. Spread to the edges with a rubber spatula. Sprinkle the chopped walnuts over the chocolate and pat down with your hands.
5. Cool and cut into squares.

ABOUT 50 PIECES

Short Takes from Ryan's Hope

Jillian Coleridge

JILLIAN'S JELLIED GAZPACHO
JELLIED GAZPACHO

1½ cups water
1 beef bouillon cube
1 envelope unflavored gelatin
¼ cup vinegar
1 teaspoon salt
½ teaspoon paprika
½ teaspoon dried basil, crushed, using a mortar
    and pestle
¼ teaspoon ground cloves
⅛ teaspoon Tabasco
1 garlic clove, minced
1½ cups finely chopped fresh tomatoes
½ cup finely chopped green pepper
½ cup finely chopped cucumber
¼ cup finely chopped celery
2 tablespoons finely chopped onion

1. Combine ½ cup of the water, the bouillon cube and the gelatin in a saucepan over low heat and stir until the gelatin is completely dissolved.
2. Remove from the heat and stir in the remaining water, vinegar, seasonings and herbs.
3. Chill until the mixture has the consistency of an unbeaten egg. Fold in the chopped vegetables and chill until firm.

4 TO 6 PORTIONS

Jack Fenelli

FENELLI'S LASAGNA
LASAGNA

2 cans (28 ounces each) Italian solid-pack
    tomatoes
2 cans (12 ounces each) tomato paste
1 large bunch of fresh parsley, chopped
1 teaspoon salt
½ teaspoon pepper
2 teaspoons orégano, crushed, using a mortar
    and pestle
½ teaspoon thyme, crushed, using a mortar and
    pestle
½ teaspoon marjoram, crushed, using a mortar
    and pestle
2 tablespoons corn-oil margarine
4 large onions, chopped
2 garlic cloves, minced
3 pounds ground beef round
3 quarts water, boiling
½ pound lasagna noodles
2 pounds ricotta cheese
1 pound mozzarella cheese
½ pound Parmesan cheese, grated

1. Combine the tomatoes and tomato paste, parsley and seasonings and herbs in a large deep skillet and bring to a boil. Reduce the heat and simmer.
2. Heat the margarine in another skillet and sauté the chopped onion until brown. Add the minced garlic and stir well.
3. In a third large skillet, sauté the ground beef until done. Add the browned onions and garlic and the tomato mixture. Mix well and continue to simmer.
4. Cook the lasagna noodles in 3 quarts boiling water for 10 to 12 minutes. Drain and rinse with cold water in a colander.
5. Cover the bottom of a large flat casserole, 9 x 13 inches and at least 2 inches deep, with a ¼-inch layer of the sauce. Add a layer of the lasagna noodles, trimming the edges to fit the dish. On top of this put a layer of ricotta cheese, a layer of mozzarella cheese and a layer of Parmesan cheese. Repeat until the casserole is filled. The top layer should be sauce, sprinkled with Parmesan cheese.
6. Bake in a 350°F. oven for 45 minutes.

12 PORTIONS

Jack Fenelli

JACK'S ITALIAN MEATBALLS
ITALIAN MEATBALLS

TOMATO SAUCE
2 cups canned tomato sauce
¼ cup chopped onion
1 teaspoon salt
Pinch of black pepper
½ teaspoon orégano, crushed, using a mortar
    and pestle
1 garlic clove, crushed
MEATBALLS
2 pounds ground beef
1 large garlic clove, crushed
1 egg, beaten
10 ounces frozen chopped spinach, thawed
2 tablespoons grated Parmesan cheese
2 teaspoons salt
Pinch of pepper
½ teaspoon ground allspice
Flour
1 pound spaghetti, cooked according to package
    directions

1. Combine the sauce ingredients in a skillet and mix well. Set aside.
2. Combine all other ingredients except the flour and spaghetti and mix well. Form into small balls and roll lightly in flour.
3. Bring the tomato sauce almost to the boiling point and add the floured meatballs. Poach, covered, but with the lid ajar to allow some steam to escape, for 1 hour. If the tomato sauce gets too thick, add a little hot water and close the lid.
4. Serve over the spaghetti.

6 TO 8 PORTIONS

Variation: Eliminate the sauce and the spaghetti and form into a meat loaf.

Jack Fenelli

MANGIA PARMIGIANA
BAKED EGGPLANT PARMIGIANA

1 large eggplant, 2 pounds
¼ cup butter or corn-oil margarine, at room temperature
¼ cup grated Parmesan cheese
¼ teaspoon salt
⅛ teaspoon freshly ground black pepper
Chopped parsley for garnish

1. Peel the eggplant and cut off the ends. Cut into 8 slices about ½ inch thick.
2. Combine the butter or margarine, cheese, salt and pepper and blend thoroughly. Spread on both sides of the eggplant slices and place them on an oiled cookie sheet.
3. Bake at 400°F. for 15 to 20 minutes, or until the eggplant is tender. Serve immediately, garnished with chopped parsley.

4 PORTIONS

Jack Fenelli

PORK CHOPS PIZZAIOLA

1 can (16 ounces) tomatoes
¼ teaspoon salt
⅛ teaspoon freshly ground black pepper
1 tablespoon olive oil
4 pork chops, 1 inch thick
4 garlic cloves, minced
1½ cups thinly sliced mushrooms
1½ cups 1-inch pieces of green pepper
1 teaspoon orégano, crushed, using a mortar and pestle
½ cup dry white wine (I like Chablis)

1. Bring the tomatoes, salt and pepper to a boil in a saucepan. Reduce the heat and simmer, stirring occasionally, until reduced to 1½ cups.
2. Heat the olive oil in a skillet and brown the pork chops on both sides. Add the garlic, mushrooms and green pepper and cook, covered, for 5 minutes.
3. Add the orégano, wine and the tomatoes. Cook, covered, for 35 to 40 minutes more. Serve with noodles sprinkled with Parmesan cheese.

4 PORTIONS

Jack Fenelli

ARRIVEDERCI ROMA CACCIATORA
ITALIAN CHICKEN CACCIATORA

1 frying chicken, 3 pounds, cut into 10 small
    pieces
1 tablespoon finely chopped fresh parsley
1½ celery ribs with leaves, finely chopped
3 garlic cloves, minced
3 tablespoons olive oil
2 bay leaves
1 cup dry white wine (Chablis is best)
¼ cup chicken broth
1 teaspoon salt
Few pinches of pepper

1. Prepare the chicken pieces and set aside. Combine the parsley, celery and garlic and set aside.
2. Heat the olive oil in a cured iron skillet or frying pan and brown the chicken for 10 minutes. Add the parsley, celery and garlic and continue to cook until celery is tender, turning everything over regularly to keep the vegetables from burning.
3. Add the bay leaves and wine and cook over high heat until the wine is almost evaporated. Add the chicken broth and mix thoroughly. Add the salt and pepper and continue to simmer for at least 20 minutes, or until the chicken is tender. Remove the bay leaf. Serve with Italian bread.

5 PORTIONS

Jack Fenelli

SWEET VEAL ROLLS
VEAL ROLLS MARSALA

2 slices of boneless veal, pounded thin (about ½
    pound)
2 slices of mozzarella cheese
2 thin slices of boiled ham (about ¼ pound)
2 tablespoons butter or corn-oil margarine
1 tablespoon flour
½ teaspoon salt
½ cup Marsala wine
Chopped fresh parsley for garnish

1. Roll together a slice of veal, a slice of cheese and a slice of ham and secure the roll with a toothpick. Repeat with the other roll.
2. Heat the butter or corn-oil margarine in a skillet and lightly brown the veal and ham rolls. Reduce the heat, cover the skillet, and cook for 10 minutes. Remove rolls from the pan and keep warm.
3. Mix the flour and salt and add to the drippings, stirring and simmering for 3 minutes. Add the wine and simmer for 1 minute. Pour the wine mixture over the rolls and sprinkle with chopped fresh parsley.

2 PORTIONS

Faith Coleridge

FAITH'S QUICK CRAB QUICHE
CRAB QUICHE

Pastry for 9-inch 1-crust pie
½ cup mayonnaise
2 tablespoons flour
2 eggs, beaten
½ cup milk
2 cans (6 ounces each) drained and flaked crab meat
8 ounces Swiss cheese, grated
⅓ cup chopped green onions

1. Prepare the pastry and place in a 9-inch pie pan or quiche dish.
2. Combine all other ingredients and mix well. Pour into the pastry-lined dish and bake at 350°F. for 40 to 45 minutes, or until quiche rises slightly in the center.

6 PORTIONS

Faith Coleridge

RAISIN' CAIN SAUCE
RAISIN SAUCE

½ cup light raisins
Hot water to cover
2 cups dairy sour cream
3 teaspoons prepared horseradish

2 teaspoons freshly squeezed lemon juice
½ teaspoon salt

1. Cover the raisins with the hot water and let stand for 5 minutes. Drain and dry on a paper towel.
2. Combine raisins with the rest of the ingredients and mix well. Refrigerate and serve with ham.

2½ CUPS SAUCE

Faith Coleridge

FOXY FRENCH DRESSING WITH CHEESE
FRENCH DRESSING WITH CHEESE

1 tablespoon dry mustard
1 tablespoon salt
1 teaspoon sugar, or ¾ teaspoon pure crystalline fructose
5 tablespoons white-wine vinegar
1 cup corn oil
¼ cup grated Parmesan cheese
2 tablespoons mayonnaise
1 garlic clove, uncut, with a toothpick stuck in it

1. Combine the mustard, salt and sugar in a bowl. Add the vinegar and oil and mix well with an electric mixer. Add the cheese and mayonnaise and continue to mix.
2. Pour into a jar and add the uncut garlic clove with its toothpick. Store in the refrigerator. Shake well before using. This is good on a tossed green salad with some anchovy fillets added; or over pear halves with cream cheese which has been rolled in chopped peanuts.

1½ CUPS DRESSING

Faith Coleridge

GREEN GODDESS DRESSING

1 garlic clove, finely minced or put through a
   press
2 tablespoons anchovy paste
3 tablespoons finely chopped chives
1 tablespoon freshly squeezed lemon juice
1 tablespoon tarragon wine vinegar
½ cup dairy sour cream
½ cup mayonnaise
⅓ cup finely chopped fresh parsley
Salt and freshly ground black pepper

1. In a bowl combine all ingredients in the order
   given, adding seasoning to taste; mix well.
   Chill. This is especially good with romaine
   lettuce.

1⅓ CUPS DRESSING

Faith Coleridge

RACY ROQUEFORT DRESSING
ROQUEFORT DRESSING

3 tablespoons sugar, or 2 tablespoons pure
   crystalline fructose
1 tablespoon salt

½ teaspoon freshly ground black pepper
¼ cup fresh lemon juice
1 onion, chopped
3 garlic cloves, minced
1 cup corn oil
8 ounces Roquefort cheese, crumbled

1. Combine the sugar, salt, pepper and lemon
   juice and blend well. Add the chopped onion,
   garlic and oil and allow to stand for at least 4
   hours.
2. Strain the mixture and add the Roquefort
   cheese; mix well and transfer to a jar with a
   tight-fitting lid, and refrigerate.

2 CUPS DRESSING

Seneca Beaulac

BEAULAC'S BUTTERSCOTCH SAUCE
BUTTERSCOTCH SAUCE

½ cup water
1½ cups brown sugar
⅔ cup corn syrup
⅔ cup evaporated milk
4 teaspoons sherry

1. Combine the water, sugar and corn syrup in a
   saucepan and bring to a boil. Cook over low
   heat, stirring constantly, until thick, about 35
   minutes.
2. Stir the milk in gradually, then add the sherry
   and blend into the mixture. Serve hot or cold
   over ice cream, gingerbread or both!

3 CUPS SAUCE

ALL MY CHILDREN

Erica Kane

I admit it—I have a weakness for midnight snacks. I love to raid the refrigerator and then whip up some exotic goodies. I guess you could say I want the best things in life; and I get them. Now I'm giving you a peek at my Midnight Snacks and Alluring Appetizers. They're a provocative prelude to a beautiful evening or a delicious way to end the perfect night. Make them for yourself and feel absolutely pampered. Or share them with someone special because they are the food of love. There's something impulsive and a little daring about setting out spiced candles and a chilled bottle of wine and wowing my current beau with my culinary talent. Which like everything else about me is extraordinary! You too can inspire ecstasy with my Oysters Sensuelle or my steaming Manhattan Clam Chowder. And what a romantic moment you create when you bring my Lovers' Fondue to the table warmed by a flickering candle flame. Dinner becomes a sensational dance between two partners, sharing hot crusty French bread and dipping fondue forks into the bubbling brandy-flavored cheese. Is it any wonder I've had more marriage proposals at dinnertime than at any other time of the day?

No one can resist the allure of my Midnight Meatballs or Passion Pâté. I make tiny pâté sandwiches on cocktail rye bread and titillate my guests with these tempting tidbits. Also a big attention getter is my Sinsational Shrimp Sauce which I serve hot or cold depending upon my mood; great as a dip, or spooned over rice or pasta. Unlike heavy meals, which I loathe, this makes a scrumptious light supper that lets me go out and dance all night if I feel like it.

But it's my Cheese Teasers that capture everyone's fancy. Just blend cream cheese and Roquefort cheese in your food processor. Then chill this tangy cheese concoction and wrap it around a luscious grape. Roll the cheese-covered grape in crushed peanuts or cashews. (The nuts will adhere to the grape since you've chilled the cheese.) What a surprise when guests bite into the cheese and discover the soft fruit center!

In summertime, I like to dine on my balcony and enjoy my superb view of New York. No less superb are two appetizers I discovered in California when I was dining in Beverly Hills. You'll adore my Hollywood Mushrooms and my Seafood Seduction, a fancy mold of succulent crab meat. (To unmold, fill the sink with warm water and dip mold carefully so as not to melt the aspic. Put a plate on the top and briskly invert.) And for something daringly different, serve my Sultry Seviche with Glamorosa Guacamole, tortilla chips and ice-cold Mexican beer for an almost forbidden delight. I know, I know! You're thinking how about my fabulous figure, how do I keep my weight down? Well, I always serve fresh fruit for dessert after this meal because where guacamole is concerned, I love to splurge.

But I do have some diet tricks. Because I model, I have to be calorie conscious. Since I'm a pushover for quiches, I make my delicate Quiche and Tell but without a crust so I cut calories. Also, the recipe calls for 2 cups of cream but I use milk to help me stay nice and slim. Quiches are terrific because you can reheat them for a late-night hors d'oeuvre and serve them with bubbly Champagne.

Diets can be dreary but I make them fun with my Banana Flirt that I mix right in my blender. The models at Sensuelle are so fond of my Banana Flirt they take it to work in a Thermos. You'll enjoy this nonfattening but filling cocktail, filled with nutritional things like yogurt and protein powder for energy. Of course, bananas are high in food value, highest in the content of potassium, vitamin A and vitamin C. Banana Flirts are a low-cal approach to a quick meal. Sometimes when I get my midnight cravings nothing else but this will do. You won't believe something so delicious can be good for you. Did you know that you can wrap bananas that are getting soft in Baggies and freeze them so you can whip up my Banana Flirt anytime?

Since even the best of evenings must come to an end, I end it with fireworks—a nearly naughty nightcap called Erica's Surprise. No one can ever seem to figure out what's in it. The luscious secret ingredients are rich vanilla ice cream and a touch of Scotch whisky mixed in a blender. The taste is so special you'll keep your friends guessing. Or try my Hot Spiced Cider to warm your nights. Perfect to curl up with in front of a toasty fire.

I guess I'm just a plain old-fashioned girl after all. I love the simple things of life—good food and someone wonderful to share it with me. Who could ask for anything more? So try my recipes and dazzle someone special; you may never be free on Saturday night again.

Erica's Midnight Snacks and Alluring Appetizers

SULTRY SEVICHE
SEVICHE OF FISH

1½ pounds firm white fish, cubed
Juice of 3 limes
¼ teaspoon garlic salt
¼ teaspoon freshly ground black pepper
2 teaspoons orégano, crushed, using a mortar
    and pestle
1 large onion, finely chopped
3 large tomatoes, peeled and diced
1 can (4 ounces) diced green chilies, drained
1 jar (2 ounces) pimientos, diced and undrained
½ cup salsa or taco sauce
Salt and freshly ground black pepper

1. Place the cubed fish in a glass dish and
   squeeze the lime juice over it. Sprinkle with
   the garlic salt and freshly ground black pepper. Cover and refrigerate overnight.
2. Add all remaining ingredients, with seasoning
   to taste. Mix well and refrigerate for 8 more
   hours before serving. Serve as a first course as
   you would serve a seafood cocktail; or use as
   an hors d'oeuvre with tortilla chips for dipping; or serve as a cold seafood salad on cold,
   crisp lettuce leaves on chilled plates.
6 TO 8 PORTIONS

HOLLYWOOD MUSHROOMS
COCKTAIL MUSHROOMS

1 can (8 ounces) button mushrooms
2 garlic cloves, sliced
2 tablespoons olive oil
1 tablespoon plus 1 teaspoon herb vinegar
1 teaspoon Worcestershire sauce
Pinch of salt
Dash of Tabasco

1. Open and drain the mushrooms, reserving the
   juice to add later. Slice the garlic into a pint
   jar with a screw top. Add the mushrooms and
   all other ingredients. Add enough mushroom
   liquid to cover.
2. Shake well to mix. Store in the refrigerator.
   Will keep for a week to 10 days.
4 PORTIONS

PASSION PÂTÉ
PÂTÉ PROVENÇALE

1 envelope unflavored gelatin
1 can (10½ ounces) beef bouillon or consommé, undiluted
2 cans (2¾ ounces each) liver pâté
1 can (4½ ounces) deviled ham
1 teaspoon grated onion
1 teaspoon freshly squeezed lemon juice

1. Soften the gelatin in the beef bouillon or consommé in a saucepan. Place over low heat and stir until the gelatin is dissolved.
2. Measure ⅓ cup of the mixture into a 3-cup mold and chill until almost firm. This makes an attractive aspic topping on the pâté mold.
3. Blend the other ingredients into the remaining broth mixture and spoon over the gelatin layer in the mold. Chill until firm.
4. Serve with crackers or cocktail rye bread as a cocktail spread.
6 TO 8 PORTIONS

GLAMOROSA GUACAMOLE
GUACAMOLE

2 large ripe avocados
2 tablespoons finely chopped onion
1 medium-size tomato, peeled and finely chopped
¼ teaspoon salt
¼ teaspoon ground cuminseed
¼ teaspoon chili powder
⅛ teaspoon garlic powder
Dash of Tabasco (optional)

1. Peel the avocados and cut them into halves. Remove the pits, reserving one of them to place in the guacamole to keep it from darkening.
2. Mash the avocados with a fork. Add all other ingredients and mix well.
3. Spoon the guacamole into a serving dish and place the avocado pit in the center. Serve as a dip with tortilla chips or raw vegetables. Guacamole can also be used as a topping on tostadas, nachos and salads. Some people even like it as a filling for omelets.
8 PORTIONS

AMERICAN BEAUTY DIP
ARTICHOKE DIP

1 can (8½ ounces) artichoke hearts, not marinated
1 can (6 ounces) marinated artichoke hearts
1 can (4 ounces) green chilies, seeded and chopped
⅓ cup mayonnaise
¼ pound Cheddar cheese, grated

1. Drain the artichoke hearts and chop into small pieces. Place in the bottom of an oiled 1-quart baking dish.
2. Cover with the chilies and then with the mayonnaise. Top with the grated cheese.
3. Bake at 350°F. for 20 to 30 minutes. Serve with tortilla chips.
6 TO 8 PORTIONS

CHEESE TEASERS
CHEESE-WRAPPED GRAPES

8 ounces cream cheese
4 ounces Roquefort cheese
2 pounds seedless grapes
1 cup crushed roasted cashew nuts or peanuts

1. Combine the cream cheese and Roquefort in a food processor with a metal blade and blend thoroughly. Place in a covered container and refrigerate until well chilled.
2. Wash and dry the grapes. Remove the chilled cheese from the refrigerator.
3. Place enough cheese to surround a grape in the palm of your hand. Place a grape in the center of the cheese and wrap the cheese completely around the grape. Place the wrapped grape on wax paper and proceed to wrap the other grapes in the same manner. When the cheese warms to the point where it is not easy to handle, place it back in the refrigerator to chill before proceeding with the rest of the grapes.
4. Spread the crushed nuts on a platter and roll the wrapped grapes in the nuts until they are completely covered. Chill until ready to serve. After they have been rolled in the nuts, they will not stick together.

ABOUT 12 PORTIONS

LOVERS' FONDUE
CHEESE FONDUE

1 tablespoon butter
1 cup white wine
½ pound Swiss (Emmentaler) cheese, grated
½ pound Gruyère cheese, grated
1 tablespoon cornstarch
½ teaspoon salt
¼ teaspoon freshly ground black pepper
⅛ teaspoon grated nutmeg
1 tablespoon brandy
French bread, cut into large cubes

1. Melt the butter in a fondue pot and coat the entire inner surface of the pot. Pour in the wine and let it warm.
2. Combine the cheeses, cornstarch, salt, pepper and nutmeg and mix thoroughly. Add by the handful to the wine and mix until creamy.

3. Stir in the brandy. Place the fondue pot over an adjustable flame (usually denatured alcohol is used in fondue warming sets) and dip the French bread into the mixture.

6 PORTIONS

MIDNIGHT MEATBALLS
MEATBALLS IN SOUR CREAM

½ pound ground beef chuck
½ cup dairy sour cream
2 teaspoons salt
¼ teaspoon black pepper
½ teaspoon garlic powder
1 tablespoon butter or corn-oil margarine
SOUR-CREAM SAUCE
1½ cups dairy sour cream
¼ teaspoon garlic powder
½ teaspoon sugar
2 teaspoons dried dill, crushed, using a mortar and pestle

Paprika for garnish

1. Combine the ground meat, ½ cup sour cream, salt, pepper and garlic powder and mix well. Form into small balls, place on a platter, and chill for at least 15 minutes.
2. Melt the butter or margarine in a skillet and brown the meatballs quickly on all sides. Pour off any fat and transfer the browned meatballs to a baking dish. Bake at 275°F. for about 10 minutes.
3. Combine the sauce ingredients. Using the same skillet in which the meatballs were browned, heat the sauce, stirring, until just bubbly. Pour any juice from the baking dish into the sauce.
4. Serve the meatballs topped with sauce and sprinkled with paprika. They are especially good with noodles or rice.

2 TO 4 PORTIONS, MORE IF SERVED AS HORS D'OEUVRE

CREAMY SHRIMP DIP

1 cup mayonnaise
½ cup dairy sour cream
2 tablespoons minced onion
2 tablespoons ketchup
1 tablespoon dry sherry
½ teaspoon Worcestershire sauce
⅛ teaspoon cayenne pepper
6 ounces frozen cooked tiny shrimps, thawed
  and drained

1. Combine all ingredients except the shrimps in a medium-size bowl and mix well. Carefully fold in the shrimps.
2. Serve at once, or cover and refrigerate for up to 5 hours before serving. This is good with raw mushrooms, zucchini slices, cherry tomatoes, celery sticks, rye crackers and many other nibbling foods.

WILL SERVE 24 AS A DIP

SINSATIONAL SHRIMP SAUCE
THREE-WAY SHRIMP SAUCE

2 cups tomato juice
2 tablespoons finely chopped onion
1 can (2 ounces) mushrooms, drained
⅛ teaspoon ground allspice
½ cup dry white wine (Chablis is best)
½ cup butter, melted
¼ cup sifted all-purpose flour

1 teaspoon seasoned salt
2 teaspoons finely ground black pepper
2 teaspoons finely chopped fresh parsley
1 tablespoon chili sauce
½ teaspoon Worcestershire sauce
2 cups small shrimps, cooked

1. Combine the tomato juice, onion, mushrooms and allspice in a saucepan and bring to a boil. Reduce the heat and simmer for 10 minutes. Add the wine.
2. Melt the butter in another saucepan. Add the flour and stir to mix thoroughly. Add the butter-flour mixture to the tomato-juice mixture gradually, stirring to blend smoothly.
3. Add the salt, pepper, parsley, chili sauce, Worcestershire sauce and shrimps and mix well. Simmer until the shrimps are heated through.
4. Serve hot or cold over rice or pasta or use as a dip.

4 CUPS SAUCE OR DIP

OYSTERS SENSUELLE
OYSTERS ROCKEFELLER

6 tablespoons butter or corn-oil margarine
2 cups chopped raw spinach
2 tablespoons chopped fresh parsley
¼ cup chopped green onions
¼ cup dry bread crumbs
½ teaspoon salt
Dash of Tabasco
2 tablespoons Pernod or anisette
2 dozen oysters on the half shell

1. Melt the butter or margarine in a saucepan and add all ingredients except the Pernod and

oysters. Cook over low heat, stirring constantly, for 10 minutes.

2. Add the Pernod. Purée the mixture in a food processor, using the metal blade.
3. Cover the bottoms of 4 baking pans with rock salt and place 6 of the oysters in each pan. (Embedding the oysters in the rock salt helps to steady the oyster shells and also protects them from the heat.)
4. Put a spoonful of the spinach mixture on each oyster. Place in a preheated 400°F. oven for 8 minutes, then place under a broiler to brown lightly before serving.

4 PORTIONS

SEAFOOD SEDUCTION
CRAB MOLD

1 envelope unflavored gelatin
¼ cup cold water
1 can (10¼ ounces) condensed cream of
    mushroom soup, undiluted
8 ounces cream cheese
1 cup mayonnaise
½ cup finely chopped celery
1 small onion, finely chopped
1 can (6 ounces) crab meat, shredded

1. Soften the gelatin in the cold water for 5 minutes.
2. Combine the soup and cream cheese in a saucepan and heat over low heat until cheese melts.
3. Add the softened gelatin and all remaining ingredients and mix well. Pour into an oiled 4-cup mold and chill for 3 to 4 hours, until firmly set.

6 PORTIONS

CAVALIER CAVIAR
CAVIAR MOLD

1 envelope unflavored gelatin
¼ cup cold water
1½ cups dairy sour cream
2 tablespoons mayonnaise
2 tablespoons freshly squeezed lemon juice
2 teaspoons grated onion
¼ teaspoon sugar
Dash of Tabasco
2 jars (4 ounces each) caviar
Salt and pepper
2 tablespoons chopped fresh parsley
2 tablespoons chopped scallions

1. Soften the gelatin in the cold water for 5 minutes. Heat 1 cup of the sour cream in a saucepan over low heat. Add the gelatin mixture and stir until the gelatin is completely dissolved.
2. Remove from the heat and add the mayonnaise, lemon juice, onion, sugar and Tabasco.
3. Rinse the caviar carefully in a strainer and dry. Add half of the caviar to the sour-cream mixture, with salt and pepper to taste. Place in an oiled 2-cup mold and chill for 3 to 4 hours.
4. Unmold on a serving plate and sprinkle with parsley. (Unmolding is simpler if you dip the mold *very briefly* into hot water before inverting it on the serving plate.)
5. Combine remaining ½ cup sour cream, the other jar of caviar and the scallions, and spoon either on top of the caviar mold or around the edges. Serve with crackers or Melba toast.

6 PORTIONS

ASPIC D'AMOUR
VEGETABLE JUICE ASPIC

1½ cups tomato or V-8 juice
½ cup consommé
½ bay leaf
1 large celery rib
1 small garlic clove, minced
1 small whole onion
⅛ teaspoon basil, crushed using a mortar and pestle
½ teaspoon Worcestershire sauce
Dash of Tabasco
½ teaspoon salt
1 tablespoon grated onion
1 tablespoon vinegar
1 envelope unflavored gelatin
½ cup cold water

1. Combine all ingredients except the gelatin and cold water in a saucepan and bring to a boil. Reduce the heat and simmer for 45 minutes, stirring occasionally.
2. Soften the gelatin in the cold water and add to the mixture, stirring thoroughly.
3. Strain into a 3-cup mold (or 4 individual molds) and chill in the refrigerator.

4 PORTIONS

MANHATTAN CLAM CHOWDER

2½ cups canned clams with juice
3 slices of bacon, chopped
1 cup finely chopped onion
2 garlic cloves, minced
3 tablespoons flour
¼ cup dry vermouth
2 cups diced raw potatoes
1 can (29 ounces) tomatoes, undrained
½ cup finely chopped green pepper
2 celery ribs with leaves, chopped
½ bay leaf
¼ cup ketchup
3 tablespoons butter

1. Drain the clams and reserve the juice. Add enough water to the clam juice to make 3 cups of liquid and pour into a saucepan set over low heat. Chop the clams and set aside.
2. Place the chopped bacon in a large skillet and cook until crisp. Add the onion and garlic and sauté over low heat with the bacon for 5 minutes. Add the flour and stir well.
3. Add the hot clam juice and water and the vermouth to the bacon-flour mixture in the skillet, stirring constantly. Add the vegetables, bay leaf and ketchup and mix well. Cover and simmer until the potatoes are done. Add the clams and heat through.
4. Add the butter and simmer for 3 minutes more. Remove the bay leaf. Pour into hot soup plates and serve immediately.

8 PORTIONS

QUICHE AND TELL
SHRIMP QUICHE

1½ cups cooked shelled shrimps
2 tablespoons finely chopped onion
2 tablespoons sherry
4 eggs, lightly beaten
2 cups cream or milk
½ teaspoon salt
¼ teaspoon white pepper
¼ teaspoon grated nutmeg

1. Combine the shrimps with the onion and sherry and refrigerate for 1 hour.
2. Preheat oven to 450°F. Oil a 9-inch pie plate or quiche dish and sprinkle the shrimp mixture into the dish.

3. Combine the eggs, cream, salt, pepper and nutmeg and strain through a sieve over the shrimp mixture.
4. Bake at 450°F. for 15 minutes; reduce the temperature to 350°F. and bake until a knife inserted in the center comes out clean, about 10 minutes longer.

4 TO 6 PORTIONS

Variation: Line a 9-inch pie plate or quiche dish with pastry and bake at 450°F. for 5 minutes before placing the filling in the crust.

ERICA'S SURPRISE
SOFT ICE CREAM WITH WHISKY

1 pint vanilla ice cream, softened for blending
2 tablespoons Scotch whisky

1. Combine the soft ice cream and the Scotch whisky in a blender container and blend until frothy.
2. Serve in chilled wineglasses for an unusual approach to dessert and after-dinner liqueur combined. Ask your guests what is in it; no one will guess correctly! (If you want to make less, it's 1 tablespoon of Scotch per cup of ice cream.)

2 PORTIONS

HOT SPICED CIDER

This is a wonderful warm-up beverage for cold evenings and a festive drink to serve during winter holidays. It is also good cold. If you plan to serve it cold, put the lemon slices in the cider while it is still hot and cool to room temperature. Then refrigerate until cold. Cold cider is good served with a dash of soda water.

4 cups apple cider
1 teaspoon whole cloves
1 teaspoon whole allspice
2 cinnamon sticks, broken into halves
½ teaspoon vanilla extract
4 thin slices of lemon including the peel

1. Combine all ingredients except the lemon slices in a saucepan with a lid. Bring the mixture to a boil and reduce the heat to simmer. Cover and continue to simmer for 20 minutes.
2. Remove the spices if desired. Serve in mugs garnished with lemon slices.

4 PORTIONS

BANANA FLIRT
BANANA PROTEIN SHAKE

This is a wonderful high-energy "pick-me-up" or low-calorie meal replacement. It is also an excellent way to keep any bananas you have from spoiling. When you can see they should be used, you can slice them thinly, place them in Baggies and tightly close them, keeping them in the freezer for future Banana Flirts.

1 banana, peeled
½ cup liquid nonfat milk
¼ cup plain nonfat yogurt
1 teaspoon vanilla extract
1 tablespoon protein powder
Ground cinnamon for garnish (optional)

1. Combine all ingredients except the cinnamon in a blender container and blend until completely smooth.
2. Pour into a glass (or Thermos if you are taking it with you) and sprinkle a little cinnamon on the top if desired.

1 PORTION

Opal Gardner's Hearty Homecookin'

VEAL MEDLEY
VEAL WITH BEER AND PEANUTS

2 pounds veal cutlets
Flour to coat the veal
3 tablespoons butter or corn-oil margarine
1 can (16 ounces) beer
1 package (2¾ ounces) onion soup mix
1 cup sliced fresh mushrooms
1½ cups raw rice, cooked according to package
   directions
½ cup chopped peanuts

1. Shake the flour over the veal to cover all surfaces. Melt 2 tablespoons of the butter or margarine in a skillet and sauté the veal lightly.
2. Combine the beer and soup mix and add to the skillet. Bring to a boil. Reduce the heat and simmer until the veal is tender.
3. Melt remaining tablespoon of butter or margarine in a saucepan and sauté the mushrooms until tender.
4. Serve the veal over rice, with the mushrooms and peanuts sprinkled over the top.

6 TO 8 PORTIONS

BAA-BAA BARBECUE
BARBECUED BUTTERFLIED LEG OF LAMB

1 leg of lamb, about 6 pounds, butterflied
RED-WINE MARINADE
2 cups red wine
¼ teaspoon freshly ground black pepper
1 teaspoon salt
1 teaspoon poultry seasoning
3 garlic cloves, minced

1. Marinate the leg of lamb in the marinade for 24 hours.
2. Barbecue over hot coals, starting with the skin side down and turning regularly, for 1 hour, or until done to your taste.

8 TO 12 PORTIONS

CROCKPOT DINNER FOR TWO

1 pound beef roast
1 teaspoon Worcestershire sauce
¼ teaspoon coarsely ground black pepper
¼ teaspoon garlic powder
2 new (red) potatoes, unpeeled, scrubbed and cut into halves
½ green bell pepper, seeded and cut into strips
½ red bell pepper, seeded and cut into strips
1 medium-size onion, peeled and quartered
½ cup water
¼ cup red wine (optional)
Assorted leftover vegetables, mushrooms

1. Cut the roast into halves and place in the crockpot. Pour in the Worcestershire and sprinkle with pepper and garlic powder on all sides.
2. Arrange the potatoes, peppers and onion around the meat and pour the water into the pot. Add the wine if you choose. Set pot at "Low" and plug it in. Go to work; dinner will be ready to eat when you arrive home.
3. About 30 minutes before you plan to eat, you may add any leftover vegetables, either fresh or frozen, and sliced mushrooms. Use leftover meat for sandwiches.

2 GENEROUS PORTIONS

MYSTERY MEAT PIE
BEEF AND CEREAL PIE

1 package (2¾ ounces) onion soup mix (both packets)
1 cup dairy sour cream or plain yogurt
2 eggs, slightly beaten
2 teaspoons corn oil
2 pounds ground beef round
⅔ cup whole-wheat flour
⅓ cup toasted wheat germ
⅓ cup Grape-Nuts
2 tablespoons butter or corn-oil margarine, melted

1. Sprinkle the soup mix in a large bowl and mix in the sour cream or yogurt and the slightly beaten eggs. Let stand uncovered.
2. Heat the corn oil in a skillet and add the ground beef. Cook and stir slightly with a fork until the red color disappears.
3. Sprinkle the flour and wheat germ over the onion soup and sour-cream mixture and then add the meat. Mix all ingredients except the Grape-Nuts and butter thoroughly and form into a loaf. Place in an oiled large pie pan and sprinkle with the Grape-Nuts. Pour the melted butter or margarine over the top. Bake in a 500°F. oven for 18 minutes, or until the top is crusty and brown.
4. Let stand in a warm place for about 10 minutes before cutting into pie-shaped wedges.

6 TO 8 PORTIONS

WATERMELON ROAST

3-pound watermelon-cut roast (wedge-shaped cut of rump roast, popular on the West Coast)
Pepper
1 can (10½ ounces) condensed consommé, undiluted
1 envelope (2¾ ounces) onion soup mix

1. Preheat oven to 500°F. Pepper the roast to your taste and place in a baking pan.
2. Bake in the preheated oven for 20 minutes.
3. Remove from the oven and add the consommé, mixed with the envelope of onion soup mix.
4. Return the pan to the oven and turn the oven off. *Do not open the oven door for 1 hour!*
5. Cut into serving pieces and serve the cooking juices over rice.

6 PORTIONS

COMPANY'S COMIN' MEAT LOAF
MEAT LOAF

1½ pounds ground beef round
1 cup bread crumbs
1 can (8 ounces) tomato sauce
1 medium-size onion, minced
1 garlic clove, minced (optional)
1 egg
Salt and pepper
TOMATO SAUCE
1 can (6 ounces) tomato paste
1 cup water
1½ tablespoons vinegar
1½ tablespoons prepared mustard
2½ tablespoons brown sugar

1. Preheat oven to 350°F. Combine the meat loaf ingredients, with seasoning to taste, and mix well. Place in an oiled standard loaf pan and bake for 1½ hours.
2. Combine the sauce ingredients and mix well. Baste the meat loaf with the sauce often while baking.

4 TO 6 PORTIONS

NEXT TO HEAVEN NOODLE CHILI
NOODLE CHILI

(The kids love this one!)

1 slice of bacon
1 pound ground beef
8 ounces wide noodles
1 can (15 ounces) dark kidney beans with juice
1 can (16 ounces) tomatoes with juice
1 teaspoon salt

2 teaspoons chili powder
1 teaspoon honey
1 onion, diced

1. Fry the bacon in a skillet and then add the ground beef and brown in the bacon fat, stirring frequently. Set aside.
2. Cook the noodles in salted water and drain thoroughly, reserving ½ cup of the cooking water to add later.
3. Add the cooked meat to the noodles, along with all other ingredients and the ½ cup of cooking water. Place in a covered 2-quart casserole and bake in a 350°F. oven for about 1 hour. The leftovers are great because the flavor improves overnight.

6 TO 8 PORTIONS

SAVORY HAM PIE

4 tablespoons butter or corn-oil margarine
3 tablespoons minced onion
4 tablespoons chopped green pepper
6 tablespoons flour
1 can (10½ ounces) condensed cream of chicken soup, undiluted
1⅓ cups milk
1 tablespoon freshly squeezed lemon juice
2 cups chopped cooked ham
½ cup grated Cheddar cheese
1 package (10 ounces) refrigerated buttermilk biscuits

1. Heat the butter or margarine and cook the onion and green pepper until the onion is soft. Add the flour and stir.
2. Add the soup and milk and cook until thick and smooth, stirring continuously. Add the lemon juice and ham and mix well. Pour into an oiled 4-cup casserole dish.
3. Sprinkle the Cheddar cheese over the ham mixture in the casserole. Arrange the biscuits on top of the pie. Bake in a 450°F. oven for 20 minutes, or until the biscuits are brown.

4 PORTIONS

HULA HAM
HAM WITH PINEAPPLE

1 can (20 ounces) sliced pineapple rings in
    unsweetened pineapple juice
¼ cup sherry
2 tablespoons soy sauce
1 tablespoon white vinegar
3 tablespoons corn syrup
½ teaspoon ground ginger
1 ham, 8 to 10 pounds
Whole cloves for garnish

1. Pour all of the pineapple juice from the can of
   sliced pineapple into a large jar with a tight-
   fitting lid. Set the pineapple rings aside.
2. Add the sherry, soy sauce, vinegar, corn
   syrup and ginger to the pineapple juice in the
   jar. Cover and shake well.
3. Put the ham in a large bowl and pour the
   sauce over the ham. Marinate, covered, for at
   least 2 hours and preferably overnight, turning frequently.
4. Remove the ham from the marinade and place
   in a flat baking dish with a cover. Make slits
   across the top of the ham in a checkerboard
   design. Garnish the top with whole cloves and
   part of the pineapple rings. Reserve the remaining pineapple rings to put in the sauce.
5. Cover the ham and bake in a 325°F. oven for
   2 hours.
6. Pour the marinade into a saucepan. Finely
   chop the remaining pineapple rings and add
   to the marinade; cover the saucepan. Before
   serving the ham, bring marinade to a boil and
   serve in a sauce dish to be spooned over the
   ham slices.
10 PORTIONS

PORK CHOPS BLUES
BLUE-CHEESE-STUFFED PORK CHOPS

3 tablespoons butter or corn-oil margarine
2 tablespoons diced onion
⅓ cup diced mushrooms
3 cups croutons
Salt
½ cup crumbled blue-veined cheese (Roquefort
    or Stilton)
6 double pork chops with pockets (ask your
    butcher to cut them)

1. Preheat oven to 350°F. Melt the butter in a
   skillet and add the onion and mushrooms.
   Sauté until the onion is tender.
2. Add the croutons, salt to taste and crumbled
   cheese; mix well.
3. Stuff the mixture into the pork chops and arrange them in a single layer in a baking dish.
   Bake for 1½ hours.
6 PORTIONS

RUBY RED FRANKS
CHERRY FRANKS

1 can (17 ounces) cherry pie filling
1 cup rosé or dry red wine
1 pound cocktail franks

1. Combine the pie filling and wine in a saucepan and heat slowly.
2. Add the cocktail franks and heat through.
   This makes a good emergency hot hors
   d'oeuvre.
8 PORTIONS

BEANIE WEANIE
BEANS AND WIENERS

1 can (15 ounces) kidney beans
½ teaspoon prepared mustard
1½ tablespoons brown sugar
¼ cup sherry
1 package (10) wieners

1. Preheat oven to 250°F.
2. Combine the beans, mustard, brown sugar and sherry in a 4-cup casserole and mix well.
3. Add the wieners, cover, and cook for 1¼ hours.

5 PORTIONS

GLAMORAMA GUMBO
SHRIMP GUMBO

1 can (16 ounces) tomatoes
3 tablespoons butter or corn-oil margarine
½ cup chopped onion
2 small garlic cloves, chopped
½ cup chopped green pepper
2 parsley sprigs, minced
1 bay leaf
2 cups water
½ teaspoon salt
½ teaspoon white pepper
¾ pound okra, cut into halves
1¼ pounds raw shrimps, shelled and deveined
1 can (8 ounces) tomato sauce
Steamed rice, cooked according to package directions

1. Place the tomatoes in a large kettle over low heat.

2. Heat the butter or margarine in a skillet and sauté the onion, garlic, green pepper and parsley until the onion is soft and clear. Add to the tomatoes in the kettle. Add the bay leaf, water, salt and white pepper, and cook over medium heat, stirring occasionally, for 1 hour.
3. Sauté the okra in the skillet for 3 to 4 minutes. Add okra to the kettle mixture and cook for an additional 30 minutes.
4. Add the shrimps and the tomato sauce and cook another 15 to 20 minutes.
5. Serve over steamed rice.

4 TO 6 PORTIONS

TWIST AND SHOUT SPROUTS
BRUSSELS SPROUTS AU GRATIN

1 package (20 ounces) frozen Brussels sprouts, thawed
¼ pound Cheddar cheese, cut into thin slices
½ cup butter or corn-oil margarine
¼ cup dry bread crumbs
⅓ cup chopped walnuts

1. Preheat oven to 400°F. Simmer the Brussels sprouts in a small amount of water until fork tender, for 5 to 8 minutes. Drain well.
2. Place sprouts in a buttered 4-cup casserole dish and cover with the sliced cheese.
3. Melt the butter in a saucepan and add the crumbs and walnuts, mixing well. Cook for a few minutes until golden brown. Pour over the top of the cheese.
4. Bake for 5 to 10 minutes, until lightly browned.

6 PORTIONS

CREAMY DREAMY LIMA BEANIES
CREAMY LIMA BEANS AND MUSHROOMS

2 tablespoons butter or corn-oil margarine
1 cup diced fresh mushrooms
1 shallot, or ½ small onion, chopped
½ cup cream or half and half
1 package (10 ounces) frozen lima beans, cooked
½ teaspoon flour
Pinch of pepper

1. Melt 1 tablespoon of the butter in a saucepan. Add the mushrooms and cook until they are soft, about 5 minutes.
2. Add the shallot or onion and cook for a few minutes. Add the cream and cook until reduced to half the original quantity. Add the lima beans and mix thoroughly.
3. Cream together the remaining tablespoon of butter and the flour and add to the mixture in the pan and cook until thickened. Season with pepper.

4 PORTIONS

SODA SALAD SUPREME
COKE SALAD

1 can (8¾ ounces) pitted black cherries
1 can (15¼ ounces) crushed pineapple
1 cup cold Coca-Cola
1 package (3 ounces) black-cherry-flavored Jell-O

1. Drain the juices from the cherries and pineapple and heat 1 cup of the combined juices to boiling.
2. Dissolve the Jell-O with the hot cherry and pineapple juice. Add the cold Coca-Cola.

Add the cherries and pineapple and pour into a 6-cup mold or flat pan. Refrigerate until firm.
6 PORTIONS

HOLIDAY HARVEST SPECIAL
MAPLE-BAKED SQUASH, SWEET POTATOES AND APPLES

1½ pounds sweet potatoes
2 pounds winter or acorn squash
4 tart apples
¾ teaspoon salt
¼ teaspoon freshly ground black pepper
⅓ cup cider
1 cup maple syrup
Butter

1. Peel the sweet potatoes and cut into chunks. Place in a saucepan, cover with water, and simmer for 15 minutes. Drain and set aside.
2. Peel and seed the squash. Cut into chunks. Pare, quarter, and core the apples.
3. Butter a large pot. Arrange the squash, apples and potato pieces in the pot and sprinkle with salt and pepper. Pour the cider and syrup over the top and then dot with butter.
4. Bake at 300°F. for about 40 minutes, or until the vegetables are tender and lightly browned, basting with pan juices every 10 minutes or so.

8 TO 10 PORTIONS

YUMMY YAMS IN ORANGE CUPS
YAMS IN ORANGE CUPS

6 medium-size oranges, whole
½ teaspoon grated nutmeg

½ teaspoon ground cinnamon
2½ cups mashed yams (fresh or canned)
4 tablespoons melted butter or margarine
4 tablespoons sugar, or 3 tablespoons pure
    crystalline fructose
1 teaspoon lemon extract
Orange juice to make soft potato mixture
Chopped walnuts or pecans
12 marshmallows (optional)

1. Halve the oranges and remove the pulp. Save the pulp for juice.
2. Mix all ingredients except the nuts and marshmallows and stuff into the orange cups. Sprinkle with chopped nuts.
3. Heat in a 350°F. oven for 20 to 30 minutes, until warmed through. If using marshmallows, add them for the last 5 to 10 minutes.

6 PORTIONS

MONKEY BREAD

1 cup lukewarm milk
2 packages active dry yeast (check the dates on
    the packages)
2 tablespoons pure crystalline fructose, or 3
    tablespoons sugar
⅓ cup Potato Buds
2 eggs, lightly beaten
¼ cup melted corn-oil margarine
1 teaspoon salt
3½ cups flour
Melted corn-oil margarine

1. Pour the warm milk into a large warm mixing bowl and sprinkle the yeast over the top of it. Stir until the yeast is dissolved, about 5 minutes.
2. Add the fructose or sugar, Potato Buds, lightly beaten eggs and ¼ cup margarine and mix well.
3. Combine the salt and flour. Add 3 cups of the flour mixture, ½ cup at a time, mixing thoroughly. Let the dough rise in a warm place until doubled in bulk.

4. Turn dough onto a floured board and knead it, adding the remaining flour mixture until the dough is no longer sticky and is easy to handle.
5. Divide the dough into 3 equal balls and roll them out to ⅓ inch thick. Cut into strips approximately 1 inch by 2½ inches and arrange them in a well-oiled angel-food cake pan or bundt pan in a criss-cross fashion, brushing each layer with melted margarine. When all of the pieces have been overlapped in the pan, let rise in a warm place for 45 minutes.
6. Bake in a 375°F. oven for 35 minutes.

1 LARGE LOAF

Variation: Combine ½ cup pure crystalline fructose, or ¾ cup sugar, and 2 teaspoons ground cinnamon; sprinkle the mixture over each layer just after the melted margarine is brushed on.

DYNAMITE DATE NUT RING
DATE NUT RING

½ pound graham crackers, crushed to fine
    crumbs
½ pound miniature marshmallows, chopped
    into halves
½ pound pitted dates, chopped
½ cup shelled walnuts, chopped
½ cup whipping cream, whipped

1. Combine all ingredients except the cream in a bowl and mix thoroughly.
2. Line a 4-cup ring mold with wax paper and oil the paper. Press the mixture firmly into the pan and refrigerate overnight.
3. Invert the mold onto a plate, remove the wax paper, and cut into serving pieces. Serve with dollops of whipped cream.

6 TO 8 PORTIONS

SWEET GEORGIA PEACH ROLL
FRESH PEACH COBBLER ROLL

2½ cups all-purpose flour
½ teaspoon baking powder
¼ teaspoon baking soda
½ teaspoon salt
½ cup shortening
1 cup buttermilk
3 pounds ripe peaches, peeled and sliced
2 teaspoons ground cinnamon
¾ cup sugar
1 cup water

1. Preheat oven to 350°F. Combine the flour, baking powder, baking soda and salt in a large mixing bowl and mix well.
2. Form a well in the center of the dry mixture and add the shortening. Mix thoroughly, using a pastry blender, and add the buttermilk a little at a time.
3. When thoroughly mixed, divide the dough into 2 balls. Place them on a floured breadboard and roll out to 2 pieces 5 x 10 inches.
4. Divide the peaches down the center of each dough strip and sprinkle half of the cinnamon and sugar evenly over each strip. Roll the strips like jelly rolls.
5. Put the rolls in a deep baking dish or casserole. Add 1 cup of water to the dish. Bake for 1 hour, or until golden brown on the top.
10 PORTIONS

MARSHMALLOW SURPRISE
PEACH MARSHMALLOW DESSERT

1 tablespoon cold water
32 marshmallows
1 tablespoon freshly squeezed lemon juice
1 cup thinly sliced peaches
1 cup whipping cream

1. Place the cold water and marshmallows in the top pan of a double boiler over boiling water and stir until the marshmallows are melted. Remove from the heat and pour into a bowl.
2. Add the lemon juice and peaches and mix well.
3. Whip the cream until it holds stiff peaks and fold into the mixture. Place in the refrigerator until completely chilled.
4 PORTIONS

Variation: Use your other favorite fruits when available.

APPLE OF MY EYE
CINNAMON APPLE BETTY

3 cups diced peeled apples
1 teaspoon grated lemon rind
2 tablespoons fresh lemon juice
1 tablespoon ground cinnamon
1 cup sugar or ⅔ cup pure crystalline fructose

¼ cup apple juice
3 tablespoons butter or corn-oil margarine
3 cups plain cake crumbs
Additional ground cinnamon

1. Preheat oven to 350°F. Combine all ingredients except the butter, cake crumbs and additional cinnamon, and mix well.
2. Thickly butter a 3-quart casserole. Start with the apple mixture and alternate the apple mixture with the cake crumbs, ending with a layer of cake crumbs on the top.
3. Sprinkle the top with a little more ground cinnamon.
4. Cover and bake in the preheated oven for about 1 hour and 15 minutes. Uncover and bake for 15 more minutes to brown the top lightly.
10 PORTIONS

VALENTINE'S COBBLER
CHERRY COBBLER

⅔ cup sugar
2 tablespoons plus 1 cup flour
½ teaspoon ground cinnamon
1 can (18 ounces) sour red cherries, undrained
2 tablespoons butter
1½ teaspoons baking powder
½ teaspoon salt
3 tablespoons shortening
Milk

1. Preheat oven to 375°F. Combine the sugar, 2 tablespoons flour, cinnamon and cherries and mix well. Pour into a 4-cup baking dish and dot with butter.

2. Sift remaining 1 cup flour, baking powder and salt together into a bowl. Cut in the shortening with a pastry blender, adding enough milk to make a soft dough. Roll the dough into a ball and pat to the size of the baking dish. Place on top of the liquid mixture in the dish.
3. Bake for 30 minutes, or until brown.
6 TO 8 PORTIONS

ALOHA CAKE
PINEAPPLE CAKE

2 eggs
1 can (20 ounces) crushed pineapple, undrained
2 cups all-purpose flour
1 cup granulated sugar
1 cup brown sugar
2 teaspoons baking soda
1 cup shelled walnuts, coarsely chopped
Cream-Cheese Ginger Frosting (recipe follows)

1. Preheat oven to 350°F. Beat the eggs with a rotary beater or with a mixer in a large mixing bowl until light and fluffy.
2. Add the pineapple, flour, sugars and baking soda and stir in well by hand. Stir in the walnuts.
3. Pour the batter into an ungreased baking pan 13 x 9 x 2 inches, 45 to 50 minutes, or until a toothpick inserted in the middle comes out clean.
4. Remove from the oven and cool on a rack. After the cake cools, cover it with Cream-Cheese Ginger Frosting, sprinkling the chopped walnuts on top.
12 PORTIONS

CREAMY GINGER BINGE
CREAM-CHEESE GINGER FROSTING

3 ounces cream cheese, softened
¼ cup butter or corn-oil margarine
1 teaspoon vanilla extract
2 cups powdered sugar
½ teaspoon ground ginger
1 cup chopped walnuts

1. Combine the cream cheese and butter or margarine in a mixing bowl and beat thoroughly.
2. Add the remaining ingredients except the walnuts and mix well.
3. Spread over the cake and sprinkle with chopped walnuts.

ENOUGH FROSTING FOR A SHEET CAKE 9 x 13 INCHES

HEAVENLY ALMOND PIE
ALMOND PIE WITH CREAM

1½ cups chopped almonds
3 egg whites
1 cup plus 2 tablespoons sugar
2 teaspoons vanilla extract
1 cup crisp Ritz cracker crumbs
1 cup whipping cream
¼ teaspoon almond extract

1. Preheat oven to 350°F. Toast ½ cup of the chopped almonds in the oven until lightly toasted, 8 to 10 minutes. Watch them carefully as they burn easily. Set aside.
2. Beat the egg whites until they are foamy. Add 1 cup of the sugar, a little at a time, beating after each addition. Add 1 teaspoon vanilla and continue beating until the mixture holds soft peaks.
3. Mix the cracker crumbs and the 1 cup of untoasted almonds together and fold into the egg-white mixture.
4. Spoon the mixture into an 8-inch pie plate to form a shell. Bake in the preheated 350°F. oven for 30 minutes. Cool on a wire rack.
5. Whip the cream, adding the remaining 2 tablespoons of sugar, remaining teaspoon of vanilla and the almond extract. Whip until cream holds soft peaks. Spoon the whipped cream into the cooled pie shell and sprinkle the toasted almonds evenly over the top.

6 PORTIONS

OPAL'S OATMEAL COOKIES
QUICK OATMEAL COOKIES

2 cups flour
1 teaspoon baking soda
1 teaspoon baking powder
1 teaspoon salt
1 cup white sugar
1 cup brown sugar
1 cup shortening
2 eggs
2 tablespoons water
2 teaspoons vanilla extract
1 cup raisins
3 cups rolled oats

1. Sift the flour, baking soda, baking powder and salt together into a mixing bowl.
2. Add remaining ingredients except the raisins and rolled oats and beat until smooth.
3. Fold in the raisins and rolled oats. Shape into balls or drop from a spoon. Bake on an oiled or nonstick cookie sheet at 350°F. for 8 to 10 minutes, or until cookies are lightly browned on top.

ABOUT 3½ DOZEN COOKIES

Short Takes from All My Children

Myrtle Lum Fargate

MYRTLE LUM'S CHICKEN SOUP
CHICKEN SOUP

1 stewing chicken, 4 to 5 pounds, cut into pieces
1½ quarts water
1 small onion, chopped
1 bay leaf
1½ teaspoons salt
¼ teaspoon black pepper
1 cup chopped celery
8 ounces uncooked spinach noodles
1 can (16 ounces) cream-style corn
Chopped green onion tops for garnish (optional)

1. Place the chicken, water, onion, bay leaf, salt and pepper in a large kettle and bring to a boil. Reduce the heat and simmer until the chicken is tender, about 2 hours.
2. Remove the chicken from the kettle and place on a platter. Remove the bones and cut the meat into bite-size pieces. Discard the bay leaf. Set the chicken aside.
3. Add the celery, noodles and corn to the chicken broth and simmer until the noodles are almost done, 8 to 10 minutes. Add the chicken and simmer until it is heated through. Add more salt and pepper to taste.
4. Divide into 8 soup bowls. Top each serving with green onion tops if desired.

8 PORTIONS

Nina Cortlandt

NINA'S SPLIT PEA SOUP
SPLIT PEA SOUP

1 pound split peas
2 quarts water
Ham bone (with some ham on it if possible)
1 onion, chopped
2 carrots, diced
2 large celery ribs, chopped
1 bay leaf
½ teaspoon salt
3 cups chicken broth

1. Place all ingredients in a large saucepan and bring to a boil. Reduce the heat and simmer for 4 hours; or cook it all day in your slow cooker or crockpot.
2. Remove the bay leaf and the ham bone. Place the soup in batches in a blender container and blend until smooth; or force through a sieve. Cut any ham off the bone and add to the soup.

6 TO 8 PORTIONS

Nina Cortlandt

CORTLANDT CRUNCHY PARMESAN CHICKEN
CRUNCHY PARMESAN CHICKEN

1 can (3 ounces) French-fried onions, crushed
¾ cup grated Parmesan cheese
¼ cup dry bread crumbs
·1 teaspoon paprika

½ teaspoon salt
¼ teaspoon freshly ground black pepper
1 egg, beaten
1 tablespoon milk
1 broiler-fryer, 2½ to 3 pounds, cut up
¼ cup corn-oil margarine, melted

1. Preheat oven to 350°F. Combine the onions, cheese, crumbs and seasonings. Set aside.
2. Combine the egg and milk in a bowl. Dip the chicken pieces into the egg and milk mixture and then coat with the cheese mixture.
3. Place in a baking dish 7½ x 11¾ inches. Pour the melted margarine over the chicken. Bake for 55 to 60 minutes, or until golden brown.

4 TO 6 PORTIONS

Phoebe Wallingford

WALLINGFORD CHICKEN IN CHABLIS WITH GREEN NOODLES
CHICKEN IN CHABLIS WITH GREEN NOODLES

2 frying chickens, cut up
8 tablespoons butter or corn-oil margarine
3 tablespoons flour
½ teaspoon salt
½ teaspoon paprika
1 tablespoon minced dried onion
½ teaspoon dried sweet bell pepper
1 tablespoon dried parsley, crushed, using a mortar and pestle
¼ teaspoon Tabasco
½ teaspoon Worcestershire sauce
½ teaspoon celery salt
¼ teaspoon orégano, crushed, using a mortar and pestle
1 cup Chablis wine
1 cup cream

1 pound mushrooms, sliced (4 cups)
1 package (10 ounces) frozen green lima beans, cooked
1 pound spinach noodles, cooked according to package directions

1. Simmer the chicken until tender in enough water to cover. Strain, reserving 1 cup broth. Remove the skin and bones from the meaty portions, leaving meat in fairly large pieces.
2. Melt 6 tablespoons of the butter in a skillet. Blend in the flour, salt and paprika. Add the minced onion, dried bell pepper and seasonings and mix well.
3. Combine the reserved chicken broth with the Chablis and add to the ingredients in the skillet; mix well. Cook over low heat until the mixture is smooth and thickened; cool. Stir in the cream; set the sauce aside.
4. Melt remaining 2 tablespoons butter in another pan and sauté the mushrooms until tender and golden brown.
5. Combine the mushrooms, sauce, lima beans and chicken and mix well. Serve over the hot green noodles.

8 PORTIONS

Phoebe Wallingford

PHOEBE'S GRANDE DAME SOUFFLÉ
GRAND MARNIER SOUFFLÉ

1 cup milk, boiling
2 tablespoons butter
2½ tablespoons flour
4 egg yolks
¼ teaspoon salt
⅓ cup sugar, or ¼ cup pure crystalline fructose
2 tablespoons Grand Marnier
1 tablespoon vanilla extract
5 egg whites

Pinch of salt
⅛ teaspoon cream of tartar
ICE CREAM SAUCE
1 cup melted vanilla ice cream
2 teaspoons Grand Marnier

1. Preheat oven to 400°F. Place the milk in a saucepan over moderate heat so it will be at the boiling point when you need it.
2. Melt the butter in a large saucepan. Add the flour and stir for 3 or 4 minutes. Do not brown.
3. Remove the butter-flour mixture from the heat and rapidly add all the boiling milk. Stir with a wire whisk until smooth. Return to the heat and bring to a boil, stirring constantly for 1 minute. Remove from the heat and add the egg yolks, one at a time, stirring each one in thoroughly.
4. Add ¼ teaspoon salt, the sugar, 2 tablespoons Grand Marnier and the vanilla, and mix well. (You can store batter in the refrigerator at this point to be finished later, or you can proceed immediately.) If the sauce has been refrigerated, rewarm in a saucepan.
5. Beat the egg whites in a large mixing bowl with the pinch of salt and cream of tartar until they are stiff. Put one quarter of the beaten egg whites in the warm sauce and stir them in thoroughly. Add the remaining three quarters of the egg whites and fold in carefully. Do not overmix.
6. Spoon the soufflé batter into an 8-inch soufflé dish and set it in the center of the preheated 400°F. oven. Turn the oven down to 375°F. immediately and bake for 20 minutes.
7. While the soufflé is baking, make the sauce by combining the melted vanilla ice cream and 2 teaspoons Grand Marnier; mix well. Do not refrigerate, because it will be served at room temperature.
8. Divide the soufflé into 8 servings and spoon 2 tablespoons of sauce over each. Serve immediately.

8 PORTIONS

Tom Cudahy

TOM'S GOALPOST TURKEY LOAF
TURKEY LOAF

1 turkey breast, 4½ pounds, cooked and diced
    (6 cups chopped turkey breast)
1 cup soft bread crumbs
1 cup cooked rice
1 teaspoon salt
¼ teaspoon paprika
½ cup pimientos, cut into pieces
4 eggs, well beaten
¼ cup butter or corn-oil margarine
1½ cups milk
1½ cups chicken broth
SAUCE POULETTE
1¼ cups butter or corn-oil margarine
½ cup flour
4 cups chicken broth
½ teaspoon paprika
½ cup cream
4 egg yolks
2 teaspoons lemon juice
1 pound mushrooms, sliced

1. Butter a flat baking dish, 9 x 13 inches, covering the entire inner surface. Set aside.
2. Combine all ingredients except the sauce ingredients and mix thoroughly. Shape into a loaf and place in the baking dish. Bake at 350°F. for 50 to 60 minutes.
3. While the loaf is baking, make the sauce. Melt 1 cup of the butter or margarine in the top pan of a double boiler over simmering water. Add the flour, stirring until smooth. Add the broth slowly, stirring constantly. Add the paprika. Cook until smooth and thick. Slowly add the cream.
4. Beat the egg yolks and add a little of the hot sauce mixture, stirring well. Add the egg-yolk mixture to the sauce, stirring carefully. Remove from the heat and add the lemon juice very, very slowly. If the sauce curdles, pour into a blender container and blend for a few seconds.
5. Sauté the mushrooms in remaining ¼ cup butter for about 5 minutes, and add to the sauce.
6. Cut the loaf into 10 to 12 pieces and pour some of the sauce over each serving. Sprinkle each serving with paprika if desired. This is also an excellent recipe for using leftover cooked turkey.
10 TO 12 PORTIONS

GOALPOST CRANBERRY SAUCE
CRANBERRY SAUCE

4 cups whole cranberries, fresh or frozen
2 cups sugar
1 cup water
6 whole cloves
2 cinnamon sticks
½ teaspoon salt
1 cup light raisins
4 tart apples, peeled, cored and diced
1 large onion, chopped
1 teaspoon grated lemon rind

1. Combine the cranberries, sugar, water, cloves, cinnamon sticks and salt in a large saucepan and mix well. Bring to a boil and cook for 10 minutes, stirring frequently.
2. Add the raisins, apples and onion and continue cooking, stirring constantly, for about 15 minutes, until sauce is thick.
3. Remove from the heat and stir in the lemon rind. Ladle into sterilized jars and process according to the directions provided by the manufacturers of the jars. If you want just 1 quart of sauce, make half of the recipe.
2 QUARTS SAUCE

SERVING SPOON CRANBERRY MOLD
CRANBERRY MOLD

1 envelope unflavored gelatin
¼ cup cold water
1 can (16 ounces) whole cranberry sauce
¼ cup freshly squeezed lemon juice
2 teaspoons prepared horseradish
1 teaspoon grated lemon rind
Pinch of cayenne
¾ cup cottage cheese
¾ teaspoon dry mustard
¼ teaspoon salt

1. Soften the gelatin in the cold water. Place over hot water and stir until dissolved.
2. Combine with all other ingredients and mix thoroughly. Pour into a 4-cup mold which has been rinsed with cold water. Refrigerate until set.
3. Serve with cold turkey, a hot green vegetable such as broccoli in cheese sauce and other good holiday food. Men really go for this molded salad.

8 PORTIONS

STUFFED STEAK À LA CHÂTEAU
ROLLED FLANK STEAK

12 slices of stale bread, torn into small pieces
1 onion, finely chopped
½ teaspoon ground sage
1 teaspoon salt
1 tablespoon chopped fresh parsley
1 egg
Water
2 to 3 pounds flank steak
Butter or corn-oil margarine for browning

1. Combine the bread, onion, sage, salt, parsley and egg, and add enough water to make a moist mixture.
2. Flatten the steak and pound thoroughly to tenderize.
3. Spread the bread mixture over the pounded steak and roll it, jelly-roll style. Tie or skewer to hold the roll in place.
4. Heat the butter or margarine in a heavy skillet. Place the rolled flank steak in the skillet and brown on all sides. Add 1 cup of water. Cover and simmer slowly for 1½ hours.

6 PORTIONS

PINE VALLEY POT ROAST
POT ROAST

3 to 4 pounds boneless beef pot roast
2 garlic cloves, sliced
2 tablespoons butter or corn-oil margarine
1 envelope (2¾ ounces) onion soup mix
4 cups water
3 carrots, cut into halves
2 potatoes, quartered
3 tablespoons cornstarch
¾ cup cooking juices

1. Stud the pot roast with the garlic cloves.
2. Melt the butter or corn-oil margarine in a skillet and brown the pot roast on all sides. Pour off the drippings. Put the meat in a roasting pan.
3. Combine the onion soup mix and the water and mix well. Add to the roast. Cover and cook over low heat for 1½ hours.
4. Add the carrots and potatoes. Cover and cook over low heat for 1 hour, or longer if the meat is not tender.
5. Remove the meat and vegetables and keep warm. Combine the cornstarch and ¾ cup of the cooking juices to form a paste. Add to the cooking juices and stir over low heat until thickened into gravy.

6 TO 8 PORTIONS

Jesse Hubbard

JESSE'S JUICY GOOD HAMBURGERS
SEASONED HAMBURGERS

1 teaspoon onion juice
1 tablespoon prepared horseradish
1 tablespoon prepared mustard
⅓ cup chili sauce
2 teaspoons Worcestershire sauce
1 pound ground beef round
Salt

1. Combine all ingredients, with salt to taste, in a mixing bowl and mix well with your hands.
2. Form into hamburger patties and cook over charcoal or in the broiler, or even in a frying pan.

4 PORTIONS

Variation: *Great Cheeseburgers:* Flatten out 2 patties for each hamburger and place a little of your favorite cheese in the center of one patty. Place the other patty over it and seal the edges like a tart. Grill over charcoal or broil.

Jenny Gardner

KISSIE BURGERS
HAMBURGERS WITH ONIONS

Jenny's favorite food is a hamburger. She always loved onion on her hamburgers until she got to be a teenager, and realized nobody wanted to kiss a girl with onion on her breath. A friend of her mother's told her that if she cooked the onion it would not give her bad breath. She was so delighted to find she liked sautéed onions even better than raw onions on her hamburgers and that she could eat them and still kiss her boy friends goodbye without being embarrassed by onion breath.

1 tablespoon corn oil
1 large onion, thinly sliced
½ pound ground lean beef round
Salt
2 hamburger buns, toasted
2 tablespoons mayonnaise
2 tablespoons ketchup or chili sauce
2 large tomato slices
2 large lettuce leaves

1. Heat the oil in a skillet and add the sliced onion. Cook until the onion is tender and lightly browned.
2. Remove the onion slices from the pan and set aside. Form the meat into 2 hamburger patties and cook in the same skillet used for the onion until they are cooked the way you like your hamburgers. Season with salt.
3. While the hamburgers are cooking, spread the toasted hamburger buns with mayonnaise and ketchup. Put the tomato slices and lettuce on one side of each bun and spoon the cooked onion on the other half of the bun. When the hamburger patties are done, put them on top of the onion and close the hamburger.

2 PORTIONS

Jenny Gardner

JENNY'S OATMEAL CAKE
OATMEAL CAKE

(easier than cookies)

1¾ cups boiling water
1 cup oatmeal, uncooked
1 cup tightly packed brown sugar
1 cup sugar
½ cup corn-oil margarine
2 large eggs
1¾ cups unsifted flour
1 teaspoon baking soda
½ teaspoon salt
1 tablespoon cocoa powder
1½ cups chocolate chips
¾ cup chopped walnuts

1. Pour the boiling water over the oatmeal and let stand for 10 minutes.
2. Add the sugars and the margarine and stir until the margarine has melted.
3. Add the eggs and mix well. Combine the flour, baking soda, salt and cocoa. Add to the oatmeal mixture and mix well (this will be as thick as bread dough). Add half of the chocolate chips.
4. Pour into an oiled and floured baking pan, 9 x 13 inches. Sprinkle the walnuts and remaining chocolate chips on top. Bake at 350°F. for 40 to 45 minutes. This is a very moist cake.

12 TO 24 PIECES, DEPENDING ON SIZE

Brooke Cudahy

BROOKE'S ENGLISH TOFFEE
ENGLISH TOFFEE

½ cup coarsely chopped almonds
½ pound butter
1 cup sugar
2 tablespoons water
2 milk chocolate bars, ½ pound each, chopped

1. Place the chopped almonds on a cookie sheet in the center of a 350°F. oven for 8 to 10 minutes. Watch them carefully as they burn easily. Set aside.
2. Butter a pan 7 x 11¾ inches and set aside.
3. Melt the butter in a skillet. Add the sugar and water and cook over low heat, stirring frequently, for 20 to 25 minutes. Watch the color; it should not be too light nor should the mixture become sugary.
4. About 5 minutes before the toffee is ready, melt the chocolate bars in the top pan of a double boiler over simmering water, and stir in the almonds.
5. Spread half of the chocolate/almond mixture over the bottom of the pan. Pour the toffee mixture over it; then add the rest of the chocolate.
6. Cool and refrigerate. When firmly set, cut into squares.

ABOUT 60 SMALL PIECES

Daisy Cortlandt

"SAY CHEESECAKE!"
CHEESECAKE

GRAHAM-CRACKER CRUST
1¼ cups graham-cracker crumbs (20 to 22
  squares)
2 tablespoons sugar
6 tablespoons butter or corn-oil margarine,
  melted
FILLING
½ cup sugar
2 eggs
12 ounces cream cheese, softened
1 teaspoon vanilla extract
SOUR-CREAM TOPPING
1 cup dairy sour cream
¼ cup sugar
1 teaspoon vanilla extract

1. Make the crust: Combine the cracker crumbs
   and sugar and stir in the melted margarine.
   Press the mixture firmly on both the bottom
   and sides of a 9-inch pie pan. Chill for 1 hour
   before filling.
2. Beat ½ cup sugar and 2 eggs until smooth.
   Add the cream cheese and vanilla extract and
   mix thoroughly. Spoon into the pie crust.
3. Bake at 375°F. for 20 minutes. Remove from
   the oven and allow to cool before adding the
   topping.
4. Combine the topping ingredients and spread
   over the cheesecake. Bake again at 475°F. for
   5 to 7 minutes. Cool to room temperature and
   refrigerate before serving.

8 TO 10 PORTIONS

Daisy Cortlandt

UPSY DAISY FLUFFY COCONUT CAKE
FLUFFY COCONUT CAKE

2 cups cake flour
1½ cups sugar
½ teaspoon salt
1 tablespoon baking powder
6 eggs, separated
½ cup corn oil
½ cup water
2 teaspoons vanilla extract

COCONUT FROSTING
1⅔ cups sugar
½ cup water
¼ teaspoon cream of tartar
5 egg whites
1 cup grated coconut, packed firmly

1 cup whipping cream

1. Line the bottoms of two 9-inch round cake
   pans with wax paper. Preheat the oven to
   350°F.
2. Sift the flour, sugar, salt and baking powder
   together and set aside.
3. Beat the 6 egg whites until stiff but not dry
   and set aside.
4. Beat the 6 egg yolks in a large mixing bowl
   and add the corn oil, water and vanilla gradually. Beat until well blended. Add the dry ingredients gradually. Blend until smooth.

5. Fold the beaten egg whites gently into the batter. Spoon batter into the cake pans. Bake for 15 minutes, or until the cakes spring back when touched lightly in the center. Cool on a rack. Remove the wax paper.
6. Using a serrated knife, slice each layer horizontally into 2 layers, making a total of 4 layers.
7. Make the frosting: Combine the sugar, water and cream of tartar in a saucepan and stir over low heat until the sugar is dissolved. Cook without stirring until a little of the mixture dropped into cold water forms a hard ball (242° to 252°F.)
8. Beat the egg whites until stiff but not dry. Add the syrup mixture gradually, continuing to beat.
9. Whip the cream until it forms soft peaks, and spread between the 4 layers of cake. Spread the frosting over the top and sides of the cake, and sprinkle the grated coconut over and around the cake.

8 PORTIONS OR MORE

Palmer Cortlandt

PALMER'S RICHEST RUM TORTE
RICH RUM TORTE

¾ cup sifted cake flour
¼ teaspoon salt
¾ teaspoon double-acting baking powder
4 eggs, at room temperature
¾ cup sugar
1 teaspoon vanilla extract
2 tablespoons melted butter

Confectioners' sugar
Rum for sprinkling cake layers (to your taste)
2 ounces unsweetened chocolate
1 cup butter
1 teaspoon vanilla extract
2 cups sifted confectioners' sugar

1. Combine the flour, salt and baking powder and sift together. Beat the eggs, gradually adding the sugar and continuing to beat until light-colored and thick. Fold the flour mixture in gradually. Add the vanilla extract and melted butter and stir well.
2. Grease a shallow pan 10 x 15 inches and place wax paper over the bottom. Then grease the wax paper. (This is to make certain that the baked cake will turn out in one unbroken piece after it is baked.) Pour the batter into the pan and bake at 400°F. for 15 minutes.
3. Sprinkle a cutting board or other such surface with confectioners' sugar and turn the cake out onto the sugar-coated surface. Let cool and remove the wax paper.
4. Cut the cake into 4 pieces, each 5 x 7½ inches; then split each of those horizontally with a serrated knife to form 8 layers. Sprinkle each layer lightly with rum.
5. Melt the chocolate squares in the top pan of a double boiler over simmering water, and cool. Cream the butter and vanilla extract and add the confectioners' sugar and chocolate alternately, beating well until the mixture is thick enough to be spread.
6. Spread approximately 3 tablespoons of frosting between each 2 layers and then cover the tops and sides.
7. Chill overnight. Let stand at room temperature for 30 minutes before cutting into 12 pieces.

12 PORTIONS

ONE LIFE TO LIVE

Dorian Lord
Callison

There's only one thing I like better than going to parties; that's giving them. My parties at Llanfair have been sheer masterpieces. Everywhere you looked there were vases of sterling roses, swan ice sculptures and crystal goblets glimmering with wine. Pat, Will, Edwina, Jenny, Brad—all dressed in tuxedoes and flowing gowns—gathered around my banquet table savoring my magnificent mélange of main courses, one more brilliant than the next. There's nothing like a fancy party to make you feel glamorous and special. But you can capture that same dressed-up, formal feeling in the smallest gathering, in the simplest meal. The secret, I've discovered, is recipes with flair.

My irresistible recipes have had all of Llanview buzzing. I'm happy to share my discoveries with you, but a word of advice—my recipes should come equipped with a warning: Dorian's Million-Dollar Meals could become addictive, they're just that good.

What I call the pre-dinner party blues happens to us all. You've invited a few close friends over and you want to serve something out of the ordinary, something that will delight them, something unique. But you don't want to spend hours stuffing, garnishing and worrying. And you don't want to serve just plain old chicken or roast. You arrange flowers on the table, smooth on a pretty tablecloth, but humdrum food can spoil your party mood. Well, lo and behold, they're here at last: my collection of "recipes to impress." Most of these dishes cost little time and effort to prepare but look like a million dollars!

I picked up these dishes from some of the top chefs around the world. They taught me that a meal should be orchestrated like a fine symphony— one course blending into the next until you achieve a culinary crescendo.

That's why I love to show off a bit and impress my guests with menu themes.

One of my favorites is my Russian Dinner Party. I begin the meal simply, yet always elegantly, with my Artichokes à la Russe served with a dash of caviar sauce on each plate for dipping of the artichoke leaves. That's just the overture. Then try my Lord Stroganoff accompanied by buttered noodles and Unbeatable Beets in Caraway Butter, garnished with the merest touch of chives.

Herb's favorite theme is my Oriental Evening. I've given a delightful recipe for Raveable Rumaki followed by my Extravagant Egg Flower Soup and tantalizing Wow 'em Walnut Chicken with Ginger Rice Royale. You don't need a fortune cookie to predict the success of this meal.

Now I've had lobsters flown in from Maine and *escargots* imported from Paris, but nothing makes a bigger smash than my Callison Chicken in Burgundy. These lightly browned chicken breasts simmering in a sauce of parsley, spices and wine are enhanced by the distinctive taste of celery used in the cooking. There's nothing else like it!

I've been told I can make the simple dish of cheese and crackers a culinary event, so wait until you see what I can do with fish recipes! You'll love my Priceless Poached Fish in Dill Sauce. (Always use fresh dill; I grow mine right in my garden.) Gently poaching a fish in hot, but never boiling, liquid with onion, wine and parsley seals in exquisite flavor.

Very special occasions call for my Poached Salmon Sensation with Tycoon Caviar Sauce. I make this for Herb on our anniversary with Ginger Rice Royale. To poach the salmon use my Bravo Bouillon for a wonderful lemon taste. For dessert, my Crowd Pleaser Sherried Pears cannot be outdone. This dish is the height of elegance, and you'll love what wonders you can work on a simple pear with sherry, cinnamon and sour cream.

Some of my recipes fare just as well in the daytime. I find brunch such a civilized way to start a weekend, and it's my chance to entertain business associates. Edwina loves my Riviera Curried Crab Crêpes so much she wanted to write them up in the *Banner*. I prepare tiny banana muffins the size of bonbons to go with this dish. I also like to serve my Magnificent Mushroom and Watercress Salad, topped with crunchy toasted pine nuts. I sauté the mushrooms lightly in the dressing and then spoon this sauce over the cold watercress and Bibb lettuce. It's always a bit of fun to watch the surprise on my guest's face when she takes the first bite and finds it warm rather than cold. In my continuous search for unique brunch recipes I hit upon Million Dollar Minute Steaks. These tender, wine-flavored steaks are arranged on toasted English muffins; they make brunch a spectacular achievement.

I guess you can tell by now I love to make an occasion out of even the simplest meals like our good old American tuna sandwich. When we lounge around the pool, or when Cassie comes in from a day out with her friends, I prepare her my Fancy Tuna Sandwich. Bacon gives it a terrific crisp, smoked taste; I place a bacon rosette on each sandwich and top it off with fresh peas.

I also find side dishes a marvelous challenge to my gourmet instincts. So I recommend my best offerings: Mansion Mushroom Madrilène and my creamy Continental Celery Root. Be sure you give equal importance to selecting a side dish or a soup. It's these details that can make the difference between a good party and a great party.

Don't forget that a soup is a wonderful asset to your dinner parties. Soups are vastly underrated. A soup prepares the way, cleanses the palate, and gives one time to mull over the dining experience. I have two favorite soups, Heiress Asparagus Soup and my Blueberry Bliss, a chilled soup served with a sprig of fresh mint on top. You may have a bit of trouble with these two. Because they're so delicious you won't be able to decide which one to make first.

I love gourmet meals without hours of gourmet preparation. When you prepare my special recipes, you'll enter an elite club of culinary connoisseurs who fully intend every meal to be a dining delight.

Dorian's Million-Dollar Meals

RAVEABLE RUMAKI

20 slices of water chestnut, ¼ inch thick
⅓ cup port wine
1 pound chicken livers
Soy sauce
1 tablespoon corn oil
20 bacon slices

1. Marinate the water chestnut slices in the wine for 1 hour before you plan to make the rumaki.
2. Cut the chicken livers into 20 pieces. Sprinkle soy sauce generously on the liver pieces.
3. Heat the corn oil in a skillet and sauté the chicken livers lightly.
4. Wrap a piece of chicken liver and a water chestnut slice in a slice of bacon and secure with wooden food pick or metal skewer. Repeat.
5. Place under a broiler and cook slowly until the bacon is crisp. Serve immediately.

20 PIECES, ABOUT 5 PORTIONS

ENTRÉE CRÊPES

1 cup milk
¾ cup sifted all-purpose flour
¼ teaspoon salt
2 large eggs, slightly beaten
½ teaspoon butter or corn-oil margarine

1. Combine the milk, flour, salt and eggs in a bowl and beat with an egg beater until well mixed.
2. Melt the butter or margarine in a medium-size skillet or crêpe pan and pour 2 tablespoons of the batter into the skillet. Cook until browned on one side, grasping the handle of the skillet in your right hand and rolling the pan around quickly to spread the batter over the bottom. Turn and brown the other side.
3. Repeat until all of the batter has been used. Keep the baked crêpes in a covered warm casserole as you are finishing the others. If they are kept warm, they will remain pliable.

12 CRÊPES

RIVIERA CURRIED CRAB CRÊPES
CURRIED CRAB CRÊPES

10 Crêpes (recipe follows)
1 tablespoon butter or corn-oil margarine
1 teaspoon chopped shallot
1 can (6 ounces) crab meat, drained and flaked
½ cup dry white wine (I prefer Chablis)
1 teaspoon curry powder
¼ teaspoon Worcestershire sauce
¼ teaspoon salt
⅛ teaspoon freshly ground black pepper
Pinch of cayenne
1¼ cups prepared or canned white sauce
¾ cup prepared or canned hollandaise sauce

1. Prepare the crêpes and set aside.
2. Melt the butter or margarine in a skillet and sauté the shallot and crab meat lightly, for 5 to 6 minutes. Add the wine, curry powder, Worcestershire sauce, salt, pepper and cayenne and cook, stirring, for about 3 minutes.
3. Stir in 1 cup of the white sauce, mix well, and set aside.
4. Spread 3 tablespoons of the crab mixture down the center of each crêpe. Fold both sides of the crêpe over toward the center. Place the crêpes, seam sides down, in an oiled baking dish.
5. Combine remaining white sauce and the hollandaise and spoon over the tops of the crêpes. Bake at 350°F. for 10 to 15 minutes, or broil until browned on top.

5 PORTIONS, 2 CRÊPES PER PORTION

ARTICHOKES À LA RUSSE
ARTICHOKES WITH SHRIMPS AND CAVIAR

5 artichokes
½ teaspoon salt
Juice of one lemon
2 garlic cloves, halved
4 tablespoons butter or corn-oil margarine
2 cups dairy sour cream
½ cup finely chopped onion
8 ounces red caviar
2 hard-cooked eggs, shredded
2 cups cooked baby shrimps

1. Cut the tips off the artichoke leaves. Then cut the tops off flat, using a large knife. Cook the artichokes in about 2 inches of water in a stainless-steel kettle with salt, lemon juice and garlic until just fork tender, 40 to 50 minutes.
2. Drain the artichokes and slice them vertically into halves. Remove the choke and cut the stem, leaving about ½ inch of stem on each artichoke.
3. To serve, melt the butter or margarine. Add the sour cream and stir until warm. Add all other ingredients except the shrimps and mix thoroughly.
4. Combine a small amount of the sauce with the cooked shrimps and fill the cavities of each artichoke half, placing it in the center of an artichoke dish. Spoon the remaining sauce equally into the sauce depressions of the artichoke plates. Garnish with lemon wedges.

5 OR 10 PORTONS

EXTRAVAGANT EGG FLOWER SOUP
EGG FLOWER SOUP

5 cups chicken broth
1 cup frozen peas, thawed
½ cup cooked or canned diced button
  mushrooms, drained
¼ cup diced cooked chicken breast
½ teaspoon salt
2 eggs, lightly beaten

1. Bring the chicken broth to a boil in a kettle. Add the peas, mushrooms, chicken and salt, and mix well.
2. Add the beaten eggs to the boiling mixture and stir until they separate into shreds. Serve at once.

8 PORTIONS

BEYOND BELIEF BROCCOLI SOUP
BROCCOLI SOUP

½ cup chopped carrot
1 package (10 ounces) frozen chopped broccoli,
  thawed
1½ cups chicken broth
1 tablespoon butter or corn-oil margarine
½ cup chopped celery without leaves
¾ cup chopped onion
½ teaspoon salt
½ teaspoon dried rosemary, crushed, using a
  mortar and pestle
1 cup milk or cream
¼ teaspoon freshly squeezed lemon juice

1. Cook the carrots and broccoli in 1 cup of the chicken broth over medium heat for 15 minutes, or until vegetables are tender.
2. Heat the butter or margarine in a skillet and sauté the celery and onion until golden.
3. Place both mixtures in a blender container with the salt and rosemary and blend until smooth.
4. Return to the saucepan and add remaining ½ cup chicken broth, the milk and lemon juice. Heat to serving temperature.

6 PORTIONS

HEIRESS ASPARAGUS SOUP
ASPARAGUS SOUP

2 packages (10 ounces each) frozen asparagus,
  thawed
1 large celery rib without leaves, chopped
¼ teaspoon dried marjoram, crushed, using a
  mortar and pestle
⅛ teaspoon salt
Pinch of white pepper
3¼ cups chicken broth
2 tablespoons butter or corn-oil margarine
1 small onion, chopped
1 cup dairy sour cream

1. Combine the asparagus, celery and seasonings in a saucepan and cover with 1½ cups of the chicken broth. Simmer until asparagus is tender.
2. Melt the butter or margarine in a skillet and sauté the onion until golden.
3. Place the asparagus mixture and the onion in a blender container and blend until smooth. Add the sour cream and remaining chicken broth and continue to blend.
4. Return to the saucepan and heat to serving temperature, but do not boil.

6 PORTIONS

MOCK MARMITE

2 tablespoons olive oil
2 tablespoons chopped onion
1 tablespoon chopped celery
1 tablespoon chopped green pepper
1 can (1 pound) beef stew
1 cup canned red kidney beans
½ cup canned tomatoes
⅔ cup consommé
⅔ cup water
¼ teaspoon ground marjoram
Salt and pepper

1. Heat the olive oil in a skillet and sauté the onion, celery and green pepper lightly.
2. Add the beef stew and mash well with a potato masher. Add remaining ingredients and simmer for 20 minutes. Add salt and pepper to taste.
3. Divide into 4 bowls and serve hot.
4 PORTIONS

BLUEBERRY BLISS
COLD BLUEBERRY SOUP

3 cups fresh or frozen unsweetened blueberries
1 can (8 ounces) unsweetened crushed pineapple, undrained
1 teaspoon freshly squeezed lemon juice
½ teaspoon vanilla extract
1 teaspoon sugar or 1 teaspoon pure crystalline fructose
8 teaspoons plain yogurt
Fresh mint sprigs for garnish

1. Put 2 cups of blueberries in a blender container. Set the remaining cup of blueberries aside to add later.
2. Add all other ingredients except the yogurt and mint sprigs to the blueberries in the blender container and blend until smooth.
3. Add the remaining cup of blueberries to the soup in the blender and mix well with a spoon or rubber spatula. Do not blend!
4. Pour the soup into chilled bowls and put 1 teaspoon of yogurt on top of each serving.
5. Garnish each serving with a sprig of fresh mint.
8 PORTIONS

MANSION MUSHROOM MADRILÈNE
MUSHROOM MADRILÈNE

1 can (13 ounces) consommé madrilène, chilled
¼ cup freshly squeezed lemon juice
½ pound small fresh mushrooms, sliced (2 cups)
Sour cream
Snipped chives or green onion tops for garnish

1. Chill the consommé madrilène for several hours.
2. Combine the lemon juice and mushrooms and mix well. Let stand for at least 30 minutes, then pour off the lemon juice.
3. Combine the chilled madrilène and drained mushrooms and mix thoroughly. Serve in 4 chilled bowls. Top each serving with a dollop of sour cream and a sprinkle of snipped chives or green onion tops.
4 PORTIONS

LORD STROGANOFF
BEEF STROGANOFF

8 tablespoons butter or corn-oil margarine
2 cups sliced onions
4 cups (1 pound) sliced mushrooms
¼ cup flour
2 cups beef stock, boiling
1 teaspoon paprika
1 teaspoon sweet basil, crushed, using a mortar
    and pestle
½ teaspoon grated mace
½ cup sherry
4 pounds beef roast, cooked rare and cut into
    strips
2 cups dairy sour cream
Noodles

1. Melt 4 tablespoons of the butter or margarine.
   Add the onions and cook until tender. Add
   the mushrooms and cook until they are tender
   and the onions slightly browned.
2. While the onions are cooking, melt remaining
   4 tablespoons butter or margarine in another
   pan. Add the flour and cook, stirring constantly, for 3 minutes. Bring the beef stock to
   a boil and add to the butter-flour mixture,
   stirring constantly to form a smooth sauce.
3. Add the other ingredients except the beef,
   sour cream and noodles; mix well. Combine
   with the mushroom-onion mixture. Add the
   sliced beef and mix well.
4. To serve, heat the stroganoff to serving temperature. Add the sour cream and mix well.
   Serve over cooked noodles.

8 TO 10 PORTIONS

MILLION DOLLAR MINUTE STEAKS
MINUTE STEAKS AU POIVRE

4 cube steaks
1 to 2 tablespoons coarsely ground black pepper
2 English muffins, split
Butter or margarine for muffins
4 tablespoons butter or corn-oil margarine
2 tablespoons Cognac
¼ cup dry white wine
½ teaspoon salt
2 tablespoons minced fresh parsley

1. Sprinkle the steaks with the coarsely ground
   pepper.
2. Toast and butter the English muffins and keep
   warm in the oven.
3. Heat 1 tablespoon butter or margarine in a
   skillet and quickly sear the steaks on each
   side. Then add the Cognac and ignite it with a
   long match. When the blaze goes out, blend in
   the wine, remaining 3 tablespoons of butter or
   margarine, and the salt.
4. Arrange the steaks at once on the muffins and
   spoon the sauce from the skillet over the tops.
   Sprinkle with parsley and serve.

4 PORTIONS

DORIAN'S VEAL OSCAR
VEAL OSCAR

TARRAGON SAUCE
4 egg yolks
1 teaspoon lemon juice
½ cup butter or corn-oil margarine, melted
¼ teaspoon salt
1 tablespoon tarragon vinegar
½ teaspoon dried tarragon, crushed, using a
   mortar and pestle
Pinch of cayenne

¼ cup flour
4 boneless veal cutlets, each 5 ounces
2 tablespoons butter or corn-oil margarine
4 crab legs, split, or 1 can (6 ounces) crab meat
16 asparagus spears

1. Make the tarragon sauce: Combine the egg
   yolks, lemon juice and half of the melted butter or margarine in a saucepan and stir over
   low heat until the mixture starts to thicken.
2. Add the rest of the butter or margarine, stirring constantly. Remove from the heat, add
   the other sauce ingredients, and mix well. Set
   aside.
3. Place the flour in a plastic bag and add the
   veal cutlets. Shake the bag to cover the cutlets
   thoroughly with flour.
4. Heat the butter or margarine in a skillet and
   brown the cutlets on both sides. Place in a
   baking dish and cover each cutlet with 1 crab
   leg and then with 4 asparagus spears. Divide
   the sauce evenly over the cutlets and broil until brown.

4 PORTIONS

WOW 'EM WALNUT CHICKEN
WALNUT CHICKEN

¼ cup corn oil
1 cup coarsely chopped walnuts
2 whole chicken breasts, boned and cut
   lengthwise into very thin strips
½ teaspoon salt
1 large onion, thinly sliced
1½ cups diagonally cut celery slices
1¼ cups chicken broth
1 teaspoon sugar
1 tablespoon cornstarch
2 tablespoons soy sauce
3 tablespoons sherry
1 can (4 ounces) water chestnuts, drained and
   sliced
Ginger Rice Royale (recipe follows)

1. Heat the oil in a skillet and add the walnuts.
   Toast, stirring constantly. Remove and drain
   on a paper towel.
2. Place the chicken breasts in the skillet and
   sprinkle with salt. Cook, stirring frequently,
   for 5 to 10 minutes, or until tender. Remove
   the chicken.
3. Add the onion, celery and ½ cup of the
   chicken broth. Cook, uncovered, for 5 minutes, or until the vegetables are slightly
   tender.
4. Combine the sugar, cornstarch, soy sauce and
   sherry, and stir into the vegetables. Heat, still
   stirring, until the sauce thickens. Add the
   chicken, water chestnuts and toasted walnuts.
   Heat through.
5. Serve with hot Ginger Rice Royale.

4 PORTIONS

Variation: If you want to cut calories, you may
substitute mushrooms for walnuts.

GINGER RICE ROYALE
GINGER RICE

1½ cups uncooked rice (4½ cups cooked)
2 tablespoons corn oil
½ cup chopped green onions
2 tablespoons finely diced candied gingerroot

1. Prepare the rice according to package directions and keep warm.
2. Heat the oil in a skillet and sauté the chopped green onions for 1 minute. Add the candied gingerroot and the hot rice and toss lightly.

8 SERVINGS

CALLISON CHICKEN IN BURGUNDY

½ cup flour
½ teaspoon salt
¼ teaspoon freshly ground black pepper
2 pounds boned chicken breasts
¼ cup butter or corn-oil margarine
1½ cups consommé
½ cup Burgundy wine
1 teaspoon dried thyme, crushed, using a mortar and pestle
1 teaspoon dried marjoram, crushed, using a mortar and pestle
2 tablespoons chopped parsley
8 to 10 small white onions
4 or 5 celery ribs, without leaves

1. Place the flour, salt and pepper in a plastic bag. Drop the chicken into the bag and coat pieces thoroughly with the mixture.

2. Brown the chicken breasts in the butter in a skillet. Add the consommé, wine, herbs and onions, and cover with the celery.
3. Cover the skillet and cook over medium heat for 1 hour. Discard the celery before serving. Spoon the sauce over the chicken breasts on the serving plates.

6 PORTIONS

AFFLUENT SEAFOOD ASPARAGUS CASSEROLE
SEAFOOD ASPARAGUS CASSEROLE

2 packages (10 ounces each) frozen asparagus spears, thawed and cooked
1 cup cubed cooked lobster, or 1 can (5 ounces) lobster, drained and broken into pieces
1 cup shelled cooked shrimps, or 1 can (4½ ounces) medium shrimps, drained
3 hard-cooked eggs, sliced
1½ cups hollandaise sauce
½ cup dairy sour cream
¾ cup soft bread crumbs
1 tablespoon grated Parmesan cheese
1 tablespoon corn-oil margarine, melted

1. Preheat oven to 350°F. Drain the cooked asparagus and arrange in the bottom of a baking dish 8¾ x 12¾ inches. Layer the lobster and shrimps on top of the asparagus, followed by the egg slices.
2. Combine the hollandaise and sour cream and pour over the casserole.
3. Combine the bread crumbs, cheese and margarine and sprinkle over the top of the casserole. Bake at 350°F. for 20 to 25 minutes, or until heated through.

4 TO 6 PORTIONS

PRICELESS POACHED FISH IN DILL SAUCE
POACHED FISH IN DILL SAUCE

2½ pounds fresh, firm white-fleshed fish, in 1
    piece
1 cup finely chopped onion
1 cup coarsely chopped fresh parsley
1 cup finely chopped celery
1 cup dry white wine
1 cup chicken broth
½ teaspoon salt
Pinch of white pepper
1½ cups Diamond Jim Dill Sauce (recipe follows)
Fresh dill or parsley sprigs for garnish

1. Place the fish in a large saucepan. Add the onion, parsley and celery.
2. Combine the wine, chicken broth, salt and
   white pepper and mix well. Pour the wine-
   broth mixture over the fish and vegetables in
   the saucepan. If the wine-broth mixture does
   not completely cover the fish, add a little
   more wine until it does. Slowly bring to a
   boil.
3. Reduce the heat, cover and poach for approximately 8 minutes, or until the flesh of the fish
   is opaque. Remove pan from the heat and allow the liquid and fish to cool to room temperature.
4. Remove the fish from the poaching liquid and
   place on a shallow glass baking dish. Strain
   the vegetables from the poaching liquid and
   add them to the dill sauce.
5. Spoon the sauce and vegetable mixture evenly
   over the top of the poached fish.
6. To serve, place pieces of the sauce-covered
   fish on individual plates and garnish with
   fresh dill, if available, or parsley sprigs.

5 OR 6 PORTIONS

DIAMOND JIM DILL SAUCE
DILL SAUCE

1 cup dairy sour cream
½ cup mayonnaise
½ teaspoon salt
1 teaspoon dried tarragon, crushed, using a
    mortar and pestle
1 tablespoon dried dill, or 3 tablespoons fresh,
    crushed, using a mortar and pestle

1. Combine all ingredients in a mixing bowl and
   mix with a wire whisk. Refrigerate for at least
   a day before using.

1½ CUPS SAUCE

POACHED SALMON SENSATION
POACHED SALMON WITH CAVIAR SAUCE

8 cups Bravo Bouillon (recipe follows), boiling
3 pounds salmon, whole or steaks, preferably in
    1 piece
Parsley sprigs for garnish (optional)
2½ cups Tycoon Caviar Sauce (recipe follows)

1. Bring the court bouillon to a boil in a roasting
   pan or fish poacher.
2. Wrap cheesecloth around the salmon, tying
   the ends so the salmon can be lifted from the
   court bouillon when done. Place the wrapped
   salmon in the boiling bouillon. When it returns to a boil, reduce the heat and poach until done. This will take from 20 to 30 minutes,
   depending upon the thickness of the salmon.
3. Cut fish into serving pieces, and garnish with
   parsley sprigs if desired. Divide the caviar

sauce onto the serving plates or place in a sauceboat and pass to your guests.
6 PORTIONS

BRAVO BOUILLON
COURT BOUILLON

8 cups water
¼ cup white vinegar or freshly squeezed lemon
    juice
2 onions, sliced
2 carrots, sliced into rounds
Bouquet garni (parsley stalks, thyme sprigs,
    celery rib and a bay leaf, tied with a string)
12 peppercorns
¼ teaspoon ground cloves
Salt

1. Combine all ingredients, with salt to taste, in a large kettle and bring to boil, covered. Reduce the heat and simmer for 15 to 20 minutes.
2. Discard the *bouquet garni*. Strain the bouillon through a colander. Use the liquid for poaching. The vegetables can be placed in a blender container and puréed for an interesting side dish.

ABOUT 2 QUARTS COURT BOUILLON

TYCOON CAVIAR SAUCE
CAVIAR SAUCE

2 cups dairy sour cream
1 onion, finely chopped
2 hard-cooked eggs, finely chopped
4 ounces red caviar
1 teaspoon freshly squeezed lemon juice

1. Combine all ingredients in a bowl and mix well. Store in the refrigerator in a covered container until ready to use.

2½ CUPS THICK SAUCE

FILLETS OF SOLE SPLENDIDE
STUFFED FILLETS OF SOLE

2 tablespoons butter or corn-oil margarine
2 cans (4½ ounces each) shrimps, or ½ pound
    fresh tiny shrimps, cooked
1 can (4 ounces) mushroom stems and pieces,
    drained
1 large onion, minced
2 teaspoons chopped fresh parsley
8 sole fillets (about 2½ pounds)
½ teaspoon salt
Pinch of pepper
Pinch of paprika
2 cans (10½ ounces each) condensed mushroom
    soup, undiluted
¼ cup water
⅓ cup sherry
½ cup grated Cheddar cheese

1. Early in the day, heat the butter or margarine in a skillet and sauté the shrimps, mushrooms, onion and parsley until the onion is soft.
2. Sprinkle both sides of each fish fillet with salt, pepper and paprika. Onto one end of each fillet spoon some of the onion and shrimp mixture. Then roll up the fillet, fastening with a wooden pick. Place the fillets in a baking dish, 8 x 12 x 2 inches.
3. In a bowl, combine the cream of mushroom soup, water and sherry and pour over the fillets. Sprinkle with grated cheese. Refrigerate.
4. About 40 minutes before serving, heat the oven to 400°F. Sprinkle the fillets and sauce with paprika. Bake for 30 minutes, or until sole is easily flaked with a fork but still moist.

8 PORTIONS

LUXURY LEMON SCAMPI
LEMON SCAMPI

2 pounds thawed frozen or fresh jumbo raw
    shrimps
½ cup butter or corn-oil margarine
2 garlic cloves, minced
Juice of 1 medium-size lemon
½ teaspoon salt
⅛ teaspoon pepper
Chopped fresh parsley for garnish

1. Clean, devein, and refrigerate the shrimps. Do not butterfly them.
2. About 30 minutes before serving, preheat the broiler. Melt ¼ cup of the butter or margarine in a small skillet over medium heat. Add the garlic and lemon juice and simmer, stirring often, for 3 minutes.
3. Arrange the shrimps on a heatproof platter or broiler pan. Blend another ¼ cup of melted butter or margarine with the garlic butter and pour over the shrimps. Sprinkle with salt and pepper.
4. Broil about 4 inches from the source of heat, turning once, for 5 to 7 minutes.
5. Sprinkle with parsley and serve at once with the pan juices. Serve with brown rice cooked according to package directions.

6 TO 8 PORTIONS

FANCY TUNA SANDWICHES

2 teaspoons prepared mustard
¼ cup soft butter or corn-oil margarine
12 bread slices with crusts removed
1 cup shredded Parmesan cheese
2 cans (7 ounces each) chunk-style tuna, drained
½ teaspoon salt
¼ teaspoon freshly ground black pepper
1 cup frozen peas, cooked
½ cup chopped onions or snipped scallions
4 eggs
1 can (10½ ounces) condensed cream of
    mushroom soup
1½ cups milk
12 slices of bacon

1. Preheat oven to 325°F. Oil a baking dish 8 x 12 x 2 inches.
2. Combine the mustard and butter and spread on one side of each bread slice. Place 6 of the bread slices, buttered side up, in the bottom of the baking dish.
3. Reserve 1 tablespoon of the cheese for later. Combine the rest of the cheese, the tuna, salt, pepper, the peas and the chopped onions or scallions and mix well. Divide among the bread slices in the baking dish and cover with the other bread slices, buttered side up.
4. Beat the eggs in a bowl, add the undiluted soup and the milk and mix thoroughly. Pour over the sandwiches in the baking dish. Sprinkle the tops with the reserved tablespoon of Parmesan cheese. Bake at 325°F. for 1 hour.
5. Fry the bacon strips slowly until light brown. Using a fork, form curls and secure with toothpicks. Cook the bacon curls until crisp. Drain on a paper towel.
6. Place 2 bacon rosettes on top of each sandwich. Serve immediately.

6 PORTIONS

MAGNIFICENT MUSHROOM AND WATERCRESS SALAD
MUSHROOM AND WATERCRESS SALAD

DRESSING
1½ teaspoons salt
¼ cup red-wine vinegar
¼ teaspoon sugar
¼ teaspoon freshly ground black pepper
1½ teaspoons freshly squeezed lemon juice
1 teaspoon Worcestershire sauce
1 tablespoon Dijon-style mustard
1 small garlic clove, minced
¼ cup water
1 cup corn oil

4 cups thinly sliced fresh mushrooms
6 cups bite-size pieces of Bibb lettuce, cold
3 cups bite-size pieces of watercress, cold

1. Make the dressing: Dissolve the salt in the vinegar. Add all other dressing ingredients except the oil and mix well. Place in a 2-cup jar with a tight-fitting lid and add the oil. Shake vigorously for 1 full minute. Set aside.
2. Arrange 1 cup of Bibb lettuce on each of 6 plates. Sprinkle ½ cup of watercress over the Bibb lettuce.
3. Pour the dressing into a large saucepan. Add the sliced mushrooms and sauté over low heat until just tender.
4. Spoon the hot mushrooms and dressing over the salads and serve immediately.

8 PORTIONS

CONTINENTAL CELERY ROOT
CREAMED CELERY ROOT

This is a delicious accompaniment for any meat, fish or poultry; or you can add chopped meat, fish or poultry to the Creamed Celery Root and serve it for an entrée. It is pretty garnished with fresh dill.

2 medium-size celery roots
1 cup cream
1 teaspoon salt
1 teaspoon dillweed, crushed, using a mortar and pestle
¼ teaspoon dried tarragon, crushed, using a mortar and pestle
Pinch of white pepper
Fresh dill for garnish (optional)

1. Peel the celery roots and cut them into small pieces. Place in a steamer basket and steam, covered, over rapidly boiling water, for about 10 minutes, or until soft enough to mash easily.
2. Remove from the steamer and put in a food processor with a metal blade or in a blender container. Add all other ingredients and blend until completely smooth.

8 PORTIONS

UNBEATABLE BEETS IN CARAWAY BUTTER
BEETS IN CARAWAY BUTTER

3 tablespoons butter
½ teaspoon soy sauce
1 teaspoon caraway seeds
4 cans (40) extra small (size #3) canned beets
30 chives for garnish

1. Melt the butter in a large skillet. Add the soy sauce and caraway seeds and mix thoroughly.
2. Drain the beets and add to the caraway butter. Heat slowly, stirring frequently, until thoroughly heated.
3. To serve, place 4 beets on each plate and garnish with 3 chives arranged to look like leaves coming out from the beets.

10 PORTIONS

FOURTEEN-CARAT GOLDS
PICKLED CARROT STRIPS

1 pound small carrots, cut into strips
1 cup sugar, or ⅔ cup pure crystalline fructose
1½ cups white vinegar
1 teaspoon whole cloves
2 cinnamon sticks, broken into halves
2 bay leaves
6 peppercorns
1½ teaspoons salt
Dash of Tabasco
4 watercress sprigs, broken in pieces

1. Place the carrot strips in a steamer basket and steam over boiling water for about 3 minutes. Remove the basket and hold under cold running water for 1 minute. Drain thoroughly. Place carrot strips in jars or a heatproof refrigerator container.
2. Combine all remaining ingredients in a saucepan and bring to a boil. Pour the hot syrup over the carrot strips. Cool, cover, and store in the refrigerator.

ABOUT 2 CUPS PICKLES

BRAG ABOUT BANANA MUFFINS
BANANA MUFFINS

1 cup sugar
½ cup shortening
2 large ripe bananas
2 eggs
1¼ cups cake flour
½ teaspoon salt
1 teaspoon baking soda

1. Cream the sugar and shortening until smooth, using an electric beater.
2. Mash the bananas and beat the eggs and combine both with the sugar and shortening. Mix well.
3. Sift the cake flour before measuring and combine with the salt and baking soda. Then sift again.
4. Combine the wet ingredients with the dry ingredients, but do not overbeat.
5. Lightly grease a muffin pan which will hold 12 muffins, and divide the batter evenly. Bake at 325°F. for 30 to 40 minutes. Lift out muffins and cool on a rack. These will freeze beautifully for future reheating.

12 MUFFINS

CROWD PLEASER SHERRIED PEARS
PEARS POACHED IN SHERRY

4 firm ripe pears
2 cups water
2¼ cups sherry
¾ cup sugar, or ½ cup pure crystalline fructose
1 teaspoon ground cinnamon
1 cup dairy sour cream
Ground nutmeg for garnish (optional)

1. Peel the pears carefully, leaving the stems intact. With an apple corer remove the core from the end opposite the stem.
2. Combine the water, 2 cups sherry, the sugar or fructose and cinnamon in a saucepan and bring to a slow boil. Place the pears in the simmering syrup and cook, turning frequently, for about 10 minutes, or until pears are easily pierced with a fork but not soft. Remove from the heat and let cool to room temperature in the syrup. Cover and refrigerate all day or overnight in the syrup.
3. Combine the sour cream and remaining ¼ cup sherry and mix well with a whisk or in a blender container. Refrigerate.
4. To serve, place each pear on a plate or in a shallow bowl and spoon ¼ cup of the sour cream-sherry sauce over the top of each serving. Garnish with nutmeg, if desired.

4 PORTIONS

HERB'S STRAWBERRIES ROMANOFF
STRAWBERRIES ROMANOFF

1 quart fresh strawberries, washed and hulled
½ cup powdered sugar
1½ ounces vodka
1½ ounces light rum
1½ ounces Curaçao liqueur
½ cup whipping cream, whipped
2 tablespoons Grand Marnier liqueur

1. Sprinkle the powdered sugar over the berries. Combine the vodka, rum and Curaçao, and pour over the berries. Marinate berries for at least 1 hour, refrigerated.
2. Combine the whipped cream and Grand Marnier and fold the berry mixture into it. Wow!

4 TO 6 PORTIONS

Asa Buchanan

In Texas we do things in a big way. Why, if only 100 people show up for one of my barbecues that's a mighty small turnout. Heck, I've taken more folks on a Texas-style picnic. When we Buchanans moved to Llanview we fretted about only one thing—how could we leave all that Southern homecooking behind? Why, I was weaned on hot chili and when I learned to talk the first thing I asked for was more chicken-fried steak. So I decided to bring my good cooking with me and pass it along to you.

You'll get a kick out of my Buchanan Barn-Burnin' Barbecues and Texas Treats. You can cook meals right in your own kitchen that taste like they've just been barbecued in the backyard over a good hickory-smoke fire. Let me give you a little background on my Buchanan cuisine extraordinaire. When Clint and Bo were just little tykes we'd all pile in the car and drive down the twisting country backroads to Alice, Texas. We'd take a left off the town square and stop at a little shack tucked away in an overgrown patch of bluebells. This was the home of the most renowned victuals in Texas—the Armadillo Café. You'd walk through a screen door and into a plain old room with sawdust on the floor and 2 long pine tables and benches. Here, strangers would sit down together, take off their hats, and dig into the best food south of heaven. Folks flocked to the Armadillo from the nearby cities and we were all great pals by the time we'd finished supper. I inherited many of the following recipes from the owner and head chef of the Armadillo, Wild Bill. Wild Bill could sure cook up a storm!

First, he'd set out bowls brimming with steaming vegetables—turnip greens, black-eyed peas, butter beans and fried okra. Then someone would put a dime in the jukebox and we'd chow down his specialties—Wild Bill's Chicken Fried Steak with creamy milk gravy, Prairie Pot Roast (accented

97

with peppery ground cuminseeds). There were always plenty of pitchers of Lone Star Tea with chipped ice too. Ice tea is the most popular drink in Texas and nothing can quench a cowboy-size thirst better than this refreshing mint-spiced tea.

After dinner, the sweetest pecan tarts in creation were brought out warm and bubbling from the oven. Now I had to arm-wrestle the secret of this dessert out of Wild Bill! But one taste of my Little Bit O' Heaven Pecan Tarts and you'll see it was worth the effort. (By the way, cream cheese is the special ingredient.)

Though Wild Bill held the cooking champion title, my Sunday Barbecues were just about as rewarding as my oil wells. We'd hold them right out on the patio and we'd get two big grills heated up. Then we'd transform our picnic tables into a smorgasbord of lip-smackin', finger-lickin' good food. There'd be crescents of watermelons, Sweet and Sour Bean Salad, crocks of mouth-watering Pucker-Up Pickles. No one can believe I can take regular kosher pickles and turn them into such sweet nibblers. Then, we'd barbecue my Yellow Rose Chicken (which was marinated ahead of time in a spicy blend of lemons and Tabasco). For those steak eaters in the crowd, Bo would serve his Panhandle Steaks seasoned with vinegar. Nothing goes with barbecue like hot buttered corn on the cob. We'd grill the corn right in the husk to lock in that crisp, smoky flavor. Then as the afternoon wore on, but always before the barrel races, I'd serve my Buchanan Beer-Steamed Shrimps. I steam these right in their shells and beer gives them a unique flavor. After these shrimps cool, friends just line up to taste them and crack open the shells, tossing them in a big bowl on the table. And if my Silver Spur Shrimp Dip isn't the most scrumptious dip you ever tasted, I'll eat my ten-gallon hat.

Now all of my recipes are something to brag about. But my guests always stamp their feet and holler for my specialty, Buckin' Bronco Chili. We come to a dish that's near and dear to my heart. I make chili with a kick to it. To me the test of a good chili is if your eyes water when you take that first sweet/sour bite. For those of you who can't take the heat and prefer your chili a bit tamer, use less chili powder in this recipe. But my chili is the best for miles around and it'll sure keep you warm at night.

What party is ever complete without Bo's Macho Nachos? For you gringos in the bunch, you can either serve soft or crispy nachos. If you use corn tortillas instead of tortilla chips, you'll get the soft texture. But all nachos filled with a steaming chili and nacho cheese mixture are real Texan treasures. You'll love them!

All these dishes just lead up to the big hero of my recipe collection, Asa's Prime Rib Roast. What's so special about my prime ribs? My super secret ingredient, Sheer Ecstasy Secret Blend. Now I've got houses, planes, horses, silver and gold. But it's the recipe to this hot and spicy sauce I've got locked in my safe. Brush this delectable mixture of spices and herbs on your prime ribs and you'll taste a roast of sweet perfection.

The test of a good barbecue was if guests stayed on till dessert. When I'd put on an apron and fry up my Poor Boy Cookies there was always a full house. These treats are heated in corn oil and when cool they are dusted with a cloud of powdered sugar. I've also known friends to fight over Clint's Chocolate Cake. (This cake was my son's favorite.) Folks, this cake is so rich you'll want to insure it. Now, Bo always loved my County Fair Custard. I got this recipe when the fair came to town one summer; it's a heavenly mixture of honey, vanilla and a twang of nutmeg. This dessert is definitely a second-helping recipe and perfect to follow hearty meals.

Most times we'd have such fun at the barbecues, we'd carry the party on through the evening and start up swing dancing to a few of Texas' finest fiddle players. Of course we'd work up a whole new appetite that only could be cured by my Eggs Rancho Grande; a combination of green chilies and Cheddar cheese give this dish its western flavor. Enjoy it with a reheated slice or two of Bust Yer Buttons Bread with some fresh jam.

Yes siree, it took a lot of hard wheelin' and dealin' to get where I am today, and most of my business deals are done just sittin' down around the table with a good meal. You can tell a lot about a man by what he eats and what he serves, and I've found no one could refuse me anything after they'd tasted one of my dishes. So rustle up my recipes and turn suppertime into a good down-home cookin' jamboree.

Buchanan Barn-Burnin' Barbecues and Texas Treats

BUCHANAN BEER-STEAMED SHRIMPS
BEER-STEAMED SHRIMPS

12 ounces beer
1 pound fresh shrimps in their shells
Silver Spur Shrimp Dip (recipe follows)

1. Pour the beer into a steamer pan and bring to a boil.
2. Place the shrimps in a steamer basket above the beer. Cover and steam for 5 minutes. Remove the shrimps from the basket and allow to cool to room temperature.
3. Serve in a bowl for hors d'oeuvre, along with a bowl of Silver Spur Shrimp Dip. Also provide a dish for each person for the discarded shrimp shells.

4 PORTIONS

SILVER SPUR SHRIMP DIP
SPICY DIP FOR SHRIMPS

1 tablespoon capers
¼ cup mayonnaise
¼ cup ketchup
¼ cup prepared horseradish
Dash of Tabasco

1. Mash the capers with a fork, releasing as much of their juice as possible.
2. Combine the mashed capers and all other ingredients and mix well.
3. Serve at room temperature with Beer-Steamed Shrimps.

ABOUT ¾ CUP

HONCHO GAZPACHO
GAZPACHO

4 tomatoes, peeled, seeded and chopped
½ cucumber, chopped
1 can (29 ounces) tomato sauce
2 garlic cloves, finely minced
¼ teaspoon ground cuminseed
1 teaspoon salt
¼ cup bread crumbs
Garnishes

1. Combine all ingredients in a blender container and blend thoroughly.
2. Pour into a chilled tureen with 15 ice cubes and let stand until thoroughly chilled, adding more ice if you like.
3. Surround the tureen with small bowls of chopped tomatoes, green pepper, cucumbers and garlic croutons. Each guest can garnish his or her soup to suit the individual taste.

6 PORTIONS

ASA'S PRIME RIB ROAST
PRIME RIB ROAST

1 prime rib roast, 4 to 6 pounds
Corn oil
Secret Spice Blend (recipe follows)

1. Preheat oven to 450°F.
2. Rub the roast with corn oil and then with the Secret Spice Blend. Place a meat thermometer in the center of the roast. Place the roast, fat side up, on a rack in an open pan in the center of the oven at 450°F. for only 5 minutes. Then reduce the temperature to 225°F. and con-

tinue roasting until the thermometer registers 130° to 135°F. for rare, 140° to 145°F. for medium rare, or 160°F. for well done.
3. Remove roast from the oven and allow it to absorb juices for 30 minutes.

8 PORTIONS

SHEER ECSTASY SECRET BLEND
SECRET SPICE BLEND FOR PRIME RIB ROAST

¼ cup salt
¼ teaspoon dried thyme, crushed, using a mortar and pestle
¼ teaspoon dried orégano, crushed, using a mortar and pestle
¼ teaspoon ground cuminseed
¼ teaspoon garlic powder
½ teaspoon dry mustard
½ teaspoon paprika
⅛ teaspoon dillweed, crushed, using a mortar and pestle
⅛ teaspoon onion powder

1. Combine all ingredients in a jar with a tightly fitting lid and mix well. Store in the refrigerator.

ABOUT ¼ CUP

SMOKY OKIE BEEF RIBS
SMOKY BEEF RIBS

3 heaping tablespoons honey
1 cup boiling water
¾ cup soy sauce or tamari
4 garlic cloves, mashed
3 pounds beef ribs
½ teaspoon Liquid Smoke

1. Combine all ingredients except the ribs and Liquid Smoke in a bowl and mix thoroughly.
2. Place the ribs in a flat glass baking dish or pan with sides and pour the marinade over them. Marinate in the refrigerator for 24 hours, turning occasionally to saturate all sides.
3. About 4 hours before you plan to serve the ribs, remove from the marinade and cut into serving portions. Arrange in a large oiled casserole. Add the Liquid Smoke to the marinade and pour over the ribs in the casserole. Cover and place in a 300°F. oven for 3 to 4 hours.

4 TO 6 PORTIONS

WILD BILL'S CHICKEN FRIED STEAK WITH MILK GRAVY
CHICKEN FRIED STEAK WITH MILK GRAVY

20 soda cracker squares
2 tablespoons milk
1 egg, beaten
Salt
Freshly ground black pepper
1½ pounds round steak, ½ inch thick, cut into serving pieces
¼ cup corn oil
2 tablespoons flour
1 cup milk, heated

1. Place the soda cracker squares in a plastic bag. Using a rolling pin, reduce them to fine crumbs. Set aside in a flat dish. Combine 2 tablespoons milk, the egg, ½ teaspoon salt and ¼ teaspoon pepper in a bowl and set aside.
2. Pound the steak thoroughly to tenderize it, until it is ¼ inch thick.

3. Heat the oil in a skillet. Dip the steak into the egg mixture, then into the cracker crumbs, and place in the skillet. Brown both sides over low heat. Cover and cook over low heat for 45 minutes, or until tender.
4. Remove the meat from the pan and keep warm. Sprinkle the flour into the pan juices and cook over low heat, stirring constantly, for 3 minutes. Add 1 cup hot milk to the pan and stir until thickened. Season to taste with salt and pepper.
5. Pour the gravy over the steak or over mashed potatoes.

4 PORTIONS

BO'S PANHANDLE STEAK
PANHANDLE STEAK

3 pounds thick round steak
¼ cup bacon drippings
¼ cup wine vinegar
2 teaspoons salt
1 teaspoon prepared mustard
1 large onion, grated
1 green bell pepper, finely chopped
3 tablespoons chopped fresh parsley
1 teaspoon pepper
1 can (6 ounces) tomato paste

1. Score the steak on both sides. Combine all other ingredients except the tomato paste and marinate the steak in the mixture for 1 hour.
2. Remove the steak from the marinade and place in a baking dish.
3. Add the tomato paste to the marinade and mix well. Pour over the steak in the baking dish and bake at 325°F. for 2 hours.

6 PORTIONS

PRAIRIE POT ROAST
TEXAS POT ROAST

2 slices of bacon, diced
5 pounds eye of round beef roast, tied
3 garlic cloves, sliced
Flour
3 large onions, sliced
3 tablespoons chili powder
1 teaspoon dried orégano, crushed, using a
    mortar and pestle
½ teaspoon salt
½ teaspoon whole cuminseeds
¼ teaspoon Tabasco
1 cup beef stock
1 cup tomato sauce
Chopped fresh parsley or cilantro

1. Cook the diced bacon in a large iron skillet.
   Cut slits in the roast and insert slices of garlic.
   Sprinkle roast generously with flour on all
   sides.
2. Place the floured roast in the skillet with the
   bacon and brown well on all sides. Use a spatula to turn the roast rather than a fork. Add
   the onions and cook until they are brown.
3. Combine all other ingredients except the parsley or cilantro and mix well. Add to the skillet
   and bring to a boil. Reduce the heat, cover,
   and simmer very slowly for 2 hours. Turn the
   meat every half hour. If the sauce thickens too
   much, add more stock.
4. When the roast is tender, remove and place
   on a hot platter. Skim excess fat from the
   sauce and spoon over the roast as it is served.
   Sprinkle with parsley or cilantro.
8 TO 10 PORTIONS

LLANVIEW WEST CHILI
CHILI VERDE

8 pork chops, bones removed, meat diced
5 garlic cloves, chopped
3 onions, chopped
2 cans (8 ounces each) green chilies, rinsed,
    seeded and chopped
2 cans (16 ounces each) tomatoes, undrained
Salt and pepper

1. Brown the diced pork over low heat. Add the
   garlic, onions, chilies and tomatoes. Season
   with salt and pepper to taste. Simmer for 3 to
   4 hours.
2. Serve over red beans.
8 PORTIONS

BUCKIN' BRONCO CHILI
TEXAS CHILI

½ pound dried pinto beans
1 can (28 ounces) tomatoes
1 tablespoon olive oil
3 cups coarsely chopped green peppers
4 cups coarsely chopped onions
2 garlic cloves, minced
½ cup minced fresh parsley
2 tablespoons butter or corn-oil margarine
3 pounds beef chuck, cubed or ground
½ cup chili powder
2 teaspoons salt
1½ teaspoons freshly ground black pepper
2 teaspoons ground cuminseed
Dash of cayenne pepper

1. Soak the beans in water to cover overnight. In
   the morning, pour the beans and the water
   into a large kettle. Bring to a boil, reduce the

heat, and simmer until tender, adding water as needed.

2. Add the tomatoes and cook for 5 more minutes. Heat the olive oil in a skillet and sauté the green peppers for 5 minutes. Add the onions and cook until tender. Add the garlic and parsley and stir well.
3. Heat the butter or margarine in a skillet and sauté the beef until browned lightly. Add to the onion mixture. Stir in the chili powder and simmer for 10 minutes.
4. Add the meat and onion mixture to the beans. Add the seasonings, using cayenne to your taste, and stir well. Simmer, covered, for 1 hour. Remove the cover and cook for 30 minutes more, stirring frequently.

8 PORTIONS

BO'S SMOKY BEEF SALAMI
SMOKY BEEF SALAMI

4 pounds ground beef
¼ cup curing salt
2 tablespoons Liquid Smoke
1½ teaspoons garlic powder
1½ teaspoons freshly ground black pepper

1. Combine all ingredients in a mixing bowl and mix thoroughly. Chill for 24 hours.
2. Divide the mixture into fourths. Shape into 8-inch-long rolls and place each on a piece of cheesecloth. Roll up tightly and tie the ends with string.
3. Place the rolls on a rack in a broiler pan and bake in a 225°F. oven for 4 hours.
4. Remove from the oven and remove the cheesecloth. Pat well with paper towels to absorb excess fat. Cool slightly. Wrap in foil and refrigerate or freeze.

4 ROLLS, ABOUT 12 PORTIONS

MEXICAN BEANS AND PORK

2 tablespoons butter or corn-oil margarine
6 lean pork chops
½ onion, chopped
½ bell pepper, chopped
1 garlic clove, chopped
1 cup canned tomatoes
½ teaspoon salt
1½ pounds green beans, cut into ½-inch pieces

1. Heat the butter or margarine in a skillet and brown the pork chops on both sides. Cut pork into bite-size pieces and return to the skillet.
2. Add all other ingredients and mix well. Simmer until the beans and pork are done.

6 PORTIONS

YELLOW ROSE MARINADE FOR CHICKEN
LEMON-BUTTER MARINADE FOR BARBECUED CHICKEN

½ pound butter or corn-oil margarine
Juice of 3 small lemons
2 tablespoons salt
2 garlic cloves, crushed
1 tablespoon Worcestershire sauce
½ teaspoon paprika
½ teaspoon Tabasco

1. Melt the butter or margarine in a saucepan. Add all other ingredients and mix well.
2. Pour over chicken pieces and marinate for several hours or overnight.
3. Baste the chicken with marinade while cooking over charcoal or under a broiler.

ABOUT 1¼ CUPS MARINADE

BO'S MACHO NACHOS
NACHOS

8 ounces tortilla chips
1 can (4 ounces) diced green chilies
¼ cup chopped ripe olives
1 large tomato, peeled and diced
1 small onion, finely chopped
1 cup grated Monterey Jack cheese
1 cup grated Cheddar cheese
1 cup salsa or taco sauce
½ cup dairy sour cream
Chopped green onion tops for garnish (optional)

1. Spread the tortilla chips evenly in a baking pan 9 x 13 x 2 inches. Top with chilies, olives, tomato and onion. Sprinkle the cheeses evenly over the top. Place under a broiler until the cheese is melted.
2. To serve, sprinkle the salsa or taco sauce over the top and garnish with sour cream, and also chopped green onions if desired.
4 PORTIONS

Variation: *Soft Nachos:* Use 6 corn tortillas cut each into 6 wedge-shaped pieces; spread them evenly over the baking pan, proceeding as above.

TEXAS TOASTED RICE

1 cup uncooked rice
1 teaspoon salt
2½ cups boiling water

1. Preheat oven to 400°F.
2. Place the uncooked rice in a shallow pan with sides in the center of the oven and bake until golden brown, stirring frequently. Remove from the oven and cool.
3. Place rice in a 1½-quart casserole and add the salt and boiling water; mix well.
4. Bake, covered, at 350°F. for 30 minutes.
6 PORTIONS

EGGS RANCHO GRANDE
RANCH STYLE EGGS

½ pound Jack cheese, grated (2 cups)
1 can (7 ounces) green chilies, diced
½ pound Cheddar cheese, grated (2 cups)
4 eggs, separated
¼ teaspoon salt
¼ teaspoon freshly ground black pepper
1 can (16 ounces) whole tomatoes, drained and diced

1. Preheat oven to 350°F. Spread a layer of Jack cheese in an oiled baking dish.
2. Spread the chilies over the Jack cheese and cover with the layer of Cheddar cheese.
3. Beat the egg whites until they are stiff but not dry. Whip the yolks until they are creamy. Then combine the whites with the yolks and stir lightly. Add seasoning. Pour over the cheese and let settle into the surface.
4. Place in the oven and bake for 30 minutes. Remove from oven and add the tomatoes over the top. Return to the oven for another 30 minutes. Let stand for 10 minutes before serving.
6 PORTIONS

ASA'S BAKED BEANS
BAKED BEANS

2 cups dried small white navy beans
Water
¼ pound bacon, uncooked, strips cut into thirds
1½ teaspoons salt
¼ cup brown sugar
½ teaspoon dry mustard
3 tablespoons molasses
1 small onion, finely chopped

1. Wash the beans and rinse. Cover with water and soak overnight. Next day cook slowly until the skins burst. Drain, reserving half of the liquid.
2. Place half of the beans in an oiled casserole and half of the bacon strips on top of the beans.
3. Combine the reserved cooking liquid and all other ingredients and mix well. Pour half of the mixture over the bacon strips in the casserole. Then cover this with the remaining beans and arrange the rest of the bacon strips on top.
4. Cover the casserole and bake at 250°F. for 6 to 8 hours.
6 PORTIONS

SWEET-AND-SOUR BEAN SALAD

1 small green pepper, chopped
1 small red onion, chopped
1 can (16 ounces) cut green beans, drained
1 can (15½ ounces) yellow wax beans, drained
1 can (15 ounces) red kidney beans, drained
½ cup sugar, or ⅓ cup pure crystalline fructose
½ cup corn oil
1 teaspoon salt
½ teaspoon freshly ground black pepper
⅔ cup red-wine vinegar

1. Combine the chopped pepper and onion with the beans and mix well.
2. Combine all remaining ingredients and pour over the bean mixture. Refrigerate for several hours or overnight before serving.
8 PORTIONS

PUCKER-UP PICKLES
SPICY PICKLES

1 quart jar kosher dill pickles
1 cup sugar
1 teaspoon mustard seeds
1 garlic clove, cut into halves

1. Drain the pickles and slice into rounds.
2. Return to the jar and add all other ingredients. Cover and refrigerate for several days before using, turning the jar several times to mix the ingredients.
4 CUPS PICKLES

RODEO RELISH
BEAN AND CELERY RELISH

1 can (15 ounces) red kidney beans, undrained
⅓ cup finely chopped celery leaves
⅓ cup finely chopped red onion
⅓ cup red-wine vinegar
Salt

1. Combine all ingredients, with salt to taste, and mix gently so the beans don't bruise. Marinate for 2 hours before serving.
ABOUT 3 CUPS RELISH

BUST YER BUTTONS BREAD
BEER BREAD

3 cups stirred and measured self-rising flour
2 tablespoons sugar, or 4 teaspoons pure
    crystalline fructose
12 ounces beer
¼ cup butter or corn-oil margarine, melted

1. Combine the flour and sugar and mix with a
   spoon to blend.
2. Add the beer, one third at a time, stirring
   it in.
3. Pour batter into a lightly oiled loaf pan 9 x 5 x
   3 inches, and drizzle the melted butter on the
   top. Let the loaf sit for 10 minutes.
4. Bake in a preheated 375°F. oven for 50 to 60
   minutes, or until done.

1 LOAF

PROSPECTOR PETE'S PECAN POPOVERS
JUMBO PECAN POPOVERS

6 eggs
2 cups milk
6 tablespoons melted butter or corn-oil
    margarine
2 cups sifted all-purpose flour
1 teaspoon salt
¼ cup chopped pecans

1. Preheat oven to 375°F. Butter eight 6-ounce
   custard cups and arrange in a baking pan or
   roasting pan.
2. Beat the eggs slightly and add the milk and
   melted butter. Beat until blended, and then
   gradually beat in the flour and salt.
3. Pour the batter into the custard cups to within
   ¼ inch of the top and top each with 1 tablespoon of chopped pecans.
4. Bake for 60 minutes and remove from the
   oven. Quickly slit the side of each popover to
   let out steam and then return them to the oven
   for 10 to 15 minutes, or until their tops are
   very firm, crisp and deep brown. So the bottoms won't steam and soften, lift the popovers out of the cups to cool slightly.
5. Serve piping hot with butter. One per guest is
   usually sufficient, but some people have been
   known to eat two!

8 POPOVERS

COUNTY FAIR CUSTARD
VANILLA FLAN

4 eggs, beaten
⅓ cup honey
¼ teaspoon salt
4 cups milk
2 tablespoons rum
1 teaspoon ground coriander
2 teaspoons vanilla extract
Ground nutmeg

1. Oil a 1¾-quart baking dish and set aside. Preheat oven to 250°F.
2. Combine the eggs, honey and salt and mix
   well. Add all remaining ingredients except the
   nutmeg and again mix well.
3. Pour the mixture into the oiled baking dish
   and sprinkle with nutmeg.
4. Set in a pan of warm water in the center of the
   preheated 250°F. oven and bake for about 2
   hours, or until firm. Cool and refrigerate.

8 PORTIONS

LITTLE BIT O' HEAVEN PECAN TARTS
PECAN TARTS

3 ounces cream cheese
½ cup butter or corn-oil margarine
1 cup sifted flour
2 eggs
1½ cups brown sugar
2 tablespoons soft butter
1 teaspoon vanilla extract
Pinch of salt
1 cup coarsely chopped pecans
24 pecan halves

1. Let the cream cheese and ½ cup butter or margarine soften at room temperature. Add the flour and mix well. Chill for about 1 hour.
2. Shape into 24 balls, 1-inch size, and place in ungreased 1¾-inch muffin tins. Press the dough on the bottoms and sides to form a crust.
3. Beat the eggs, brown sugar, 2 tablespoons butter, vanilla extract and salt together. Divide the coarsely chopped pecans among the 24 tarts and spoon the egg mixture over them. Top each with a pecan half.
4. Bake at 325°F. for 25 minutes. Cool in the pan. These can be frozen.

24 TARTS

POOR BOY COOKIES

3 eggs
2 tablespoons evaporated milk
¼ cup sugar
1½ tablespoons melted butter or corn-oil margarine
1¼ tablespoons brandy
½ teaspoon salt
½ teaspoon ground cardamom seed
3 cups sifted all-purpose flour
Corn oil for deep-frying
Powdered sugar

1. Combine the eggs, evaporated milk and sugar and mix well. Add the remaining ingredients except 1 cup of the flour, the oil and the powdered sugar. Mix well.
2. Stir in enough of the remaining flour to make a stiff dough. Wrap in wax paper and chill for 1 hour.
3. Pour 2 inches of corn oil into a deep saucepan and heat to 375°F.
4. Roll half of the dough on a lightly floured board until ⅛ inch thick. Cut into 3-inch diamond shapes. Make a slit in the middle of each. Pull one corner of the dough through the slit. Fry a few at a time until just brown. Cool. Using a sifter, dust with the powdered sugar. Repeat with the remaining dough. This is a wonderful holiday recipe.

2 TO 3 DOZEN FRIED COOKIES

CLINT'S CHOCOLATE CAKE
MOCHA CHOCOLATE CAKE

2 cups sugar
¾ cup butter or corn-oil margarine (1½ cubes)
¾ cup cocoa powder
2 cups all-purpose flour
1 teaspoon baking soda
1 cup prepared strong coffee
4 eggs
3 tablespoons vanilla extract
COCOA ICING
1 pound powdered sugar
⅓ cup butter
4 tablespoons cocoa powder
2 tablespoons prepared strong coffee
4 teaspoons vanilla extract

1. Preheat oven to 350°F. Lightly grease the sides of 2 standard cake pans. Cut wax paper to fit the bottoms of the pans. If using Teflon pans, put the wax paper on the bottom, but it is not necessary to grease the sides.
2. Cream the sugar and butter together until completely smooth.
3. Add the cocoa and mix well.
4. Mix the flour and baking soda together and add alternately with the coffee.
5. Add the eggs, one at a time, beating well after each egg is added.
6. Add the 3 tablespoons of vanilla extract and again beat well.
7. Divide the cake batter between the 2 wax-paper-lined cake pans. Bake in the preheated oven for 30 minutes.
8. Remove layers from the oven and invert on cake racks to cool. Carefully remove the wax paper from the tops of the cakes. Cool to room temperature before frosting.
9. While the cakes are cooling, make the icing. Combine half of the powdered sugar with the butter and cocoa and cream together.
10. Add the coffee and vanilla extract and slowly cream the remaining powdered sugar into the icing.
11. Place 1 cake layer on a serving plate and frost the top. Place the second layer on top of the frosted cake and frost the top, and the sides of both layers.

1 CAKE (LET YOUR CONSCIENCE BE YOUR GUIDE AS TO SERVING SIZE, BUT USUALLY THIS WILL PROVIDE 8 TO 16 PORTIONS)

LONE STAR TEA
SUN ICE TEA

4 tea bags
1 gallon cold water
Fresh mint (optional)

1. Put the tea bags in a gallon glass container with a lid. Fill with water. If you wish a mint-flavored tea, add the mint sprigs. Cover and place in the sun until the tea is of the desired strength. This usually takes at least 2 hours but sometimes more, depending upon the strength of the sunlight.
2. Remove the tea bags and store the tea in the refrigerator.

16 CUPS

Short Takes from One Life to Live

Marco Dane

MARCO'S MARVELOUS MINESTRONE
MINESTRONE

½ cup dried kidney beans
¼ pound chopped ham
¼ pound chopped bacon
¼ pound chopped Italian sausage
2 garlic cloves, crushed
1 onion, peeled and sliced
2 celery ribs, diced
1 zucchini, sliced
1 leek, white part only, sliced
Pinch of ground allspice
¼ teaspoon salt
¼ teaspoon pepper
1 tablespoon dried basil, crushed, using a mortar
    and pestle

2 quarts chicken broth
2 cups shredded cabbage
1 cup red wine
1 can (28 ounces) tomatoes
½ cup uncooked elbow macaroni
Parmesan cheese for garnish

1. Soak the beans in water to cover overnight.
2. Brown the ham, bacon, sausage and garlic cloves in a cured iron skillet. Add the onion, celery, zucchini, leek and seasonings, and simmer for 10 minutes.
3. Heat the chicken broth in a soup kettle and add the skillet mixture. Drain the beans and add to the kettle, along with the cabbage and wine. Simmer until the beans and vegetables are tender, about 1½ hours.
4. Add the tomatoes and macaroni and cook for 15 minutes longer. Sprinkle each serving generously with Parmesan cheese.

6 TO 8 PORTIONS

Marco Dane

CHICKEN MARCO
ITALIAN STYLE CHICKEN

½ cup butter or corn-oil margarine
¼ cup olive oil
2 garlic cloves, minced
1 large onion, minced
4 carrots, pared and grated
¼ cup snipped parsley
1 can (16 ounces) Italian tomatoes
1 can (6 ounces) tomato paste
1 teaspoon dried orégano, crushed, using a
    mortar and pestle
½ teaspoon salt
Pepper
4 whole chicken breasts, skinned and boned
Flour to coat chicken breasts
½ pound mozzarella cheese, grated
¼ cup grated Parmesan cheese

1. Heat ¼ cup of the butter or margarine and 2
   tablespoons of the olive oil in a large skillet.
   Add the garlic, onion, carrots and parsley and
   sauté until tender.
2. Add the tomatoes and tomato paste and simmer, uncovered, for 30 minutes.
3. Add the orégano, salt, and pepper to taste
   and simmer for another 30 minutes.
4. While the sauce is cooking, coat the chicken
   breasts with flour. Heat remaining ¼ cup of
   butter and 2 tablespoons of olive oil in another skillet and sauté the chicken breasts until golden brown on both sides.
5. When the sauce is finished, place the chicken
   in the sauce and cover the top with mozzarella
   and Parmesan cheeses. Cover and leave over
   heat until the cheese is melted. Serve with garlic bread, tossed green salad and Italian wine.

8 PORTIONS

Larry Wolek

LARRY'S OLD-COUNTRY BORSCHT
OLD-COUNTRY BORSCHT

6 cups water
4 medium-size carrots, peeled and thinly sliced
4 medium-size beets, peeled and thinly sliced
2 celery ribs, cut into 1-inch pieces
1 small head of cabbage, cut into wedges
2 onions, thinly sliced
2 teaspoons salt
1 bay leaf
1 pound beef brisket, cut into 4 to 6 pieces
2 beets, coarsely grated
1 tablespoon sugar, or 2 teaspoons pure
    crystalline fructose
2 tablespoons vinegar
1 can (6 ounces) tomato paste
1 cup dairy sour cream

1. Combine the water, carrots, 4 beets, celery,
   cabbage, onions, salt, bay leaf and beef in a
   large kettle and bring to a boil. Reduce the
   heat and simmer, covered, for about 2 hours.
2. Add the grated beets and all other ingredients
   except the sour cream. Continue to simmer,
   covered, for 15 to 20 minutes. Remove the
   bay leaf. Cool soup and refrigerate.
3. Skim any fat from the soup. Bring to a boil
   over medium heat. Simmer, covered, for 10
   minutes. Top each serving with some sour
   cream.

4 TO 6 PORTIONS

Larry Wolek

CHICKEN KIEV WOLEK WITH CAVIAR AND SOUR-CREAM SAUCE
CHICKEN KIEV WITH CAVIAR AND SOUR-CREAM SAUCE

4 whole chicken breasts, skinned and boned
¼ cup butter or corn-oil margarine
2 teaspoons minced onion
Salt and pepper
2 ounces lumpfish caviar
2 teaspoons melted butter or corn-oil margarine
4 cups hot cooked rice, prepared according to
    package directions
SOUR-CREAM SAUCE
3 tablespoons freshly squeezed lemon juice
1 jar (3 ounces) sliced mushrooms, drained
½ cup butter or corn-oil margarine
1 cup dairy sour cream

1. Flatten the chicken breasts by lightly pounding them. Set aside.
2. Combine ¼ cup butter or margarine with the minced onion; season with salt and pepper to taste and mix well. Form into 4 rolls and place in the freezer until solid.
3. Preheat oven to 400°F. Remove the butter rolls from the freezer and place one in the center of each chicken breast. Spread 1 tablespoon of caviar on each butter roll and wrap the chicken breast around the butter roll and the caviar. Use a wooden pick or metal skewer in each roll to hold it together.
4. Place the chicken breast rolls in a glass baking dish and brush ½ teaspoon melted margarine over each one. Place in the oven for 10 minutes. Reduce heat to 350°F. and bake for 25 minutes more.
5. While the chicken is baking, make the sauce. Combine all ingredients except the sour cream in a saucepan and bring almost to the boiling point. Reduce the heat. Add the sour cream and mix well. Heat to serving temperature.
6. Serve the chicken breasts on cooked rice. Spoon some sauce over the top of each serving.
8 PORTIONS

Larry Wolek

WANDA'S GOULASH
GOULASH

1 pound lean ground beef
1 pound cubed beef stew meat
3 tablespoons chili powder or Hungarian paprika
1 large onion, cut into chunks
6 cups water
1 pound elbow macaroni
1 large green bell pepper, seeded and chopped
2 carrots, diced
1 can (16 ounces) whole corn, drained
1 can (16 ounces) peas, drained
1 can (28 ounces) stewed tomatoes, cut into
    chunks, with juice
1 ounce pimiento, minced
2 cans (6 ounces each) tomato paste

1. Sauté the ground beef and stew meat in a skillet with 2 tablespoons of the chili powder and half of the onion.
2. In a kettle, heat the water to the boiling point. Add the macaroni and continue to boil for 5 minutes, or until partially cooked. Do not drain.
3. Add all other ingredients to the meat mixture and mix thoroughly. Pour into the macaroni in the kettle and mix well. Boil for 15 minutes. Reduce the heat and stir and simmer for another 30 to 45 minutes. Serve hot.
8 PORTIONS

Viki Buchanan

VIKI'S COFFEE CAKE
COFFEE CAKE

3 cups sugar
1 cup butter or corn-oil margarine
4 eggs, beaten
2 cups flour
2 teaspoons baking powder
2 teaspoons baking soda
½ teaspoon salt
2 teaspoons vanilla extract
2 cups dairy sour cream
3 teaspoons ground cinnamon
1 cup chopped pecans

1. Preheat oven to 350°F. Oil and flour a baking pan 9 x 13 inches.
2. Cream 2 cups sugar and the butter or margarine together until well mixed. Add the beaten eggs and mix well.
3. Combine the flour, baking powder, baking soda and salt and add to the liquid mixture.
4. Combine the vanilla and sour cream and mix well. Beat slowly.
5. Combine remaining 1 cup sugar, the cinnamon and pecans, and mix thoroughly.
6. Pour half of the batter into the pan, followed by half of the sugar and pecan mixture. Follow this with remaining batter and then top with remaining sugar and pecan mixture.
7. Bake on the lower rack of the oven for at least 40 to 45 minutes. *Do not underbake* or the center will fall in!

12 PORTIONS

GENERAL HOSPITAL

Lesley Webber

When you were young, remember waking to the smoky fragrance of bacon crackling, fresh coffee perking and eggs sizzling in the frying pan? Even on the coldest Monday morning, the promise of a good hearty breakfast could coax the worst sleepyheads out of their warm beds.

Rick and I work hectic hours at General Hospital, and it's tempting to skip breakfast and grab a doughnut on our way out the door; but being doctors, we're well aware of the importance of a nutritious breakfast. The old cliché is true, it's not just something your mother made up: breakfast is the most important meal of the day. If you start your day with a nutritious breakfast you'll have all the energy and "fuel" needed to get you through the day. If you don't eat a little something in the morning, chances are you'll pay for it later in the day with a loss of energy.

In many active families like ours, breakfast is the only meal where the whole family is together. Because of our different schedules at the hospital we're seldom home for dinner at the same time. That's why we make the most of our mornings together and vary our breakfast menus so we never get bored.

Our breakfast recipes range from the Sunday morning elaborate to the Monday morning "I'm late" special. Now breakfast to most of us means eggs. But think of all the different ways you can prepare eggs. When dawn's early light creeps through our curtains, I whip up my Easy Eggs, which are topped with melting Cheddar cheese and baked for only 20 minutes. This is a sensational alternative to grabbing a quick cup of coffee. If you have a little more time to spare you can choose my version of Eggs Benedict, Eggs Lesley, served with crunchy Canadian bacon. Or, for a more exotic dish, try my Super Swiss-Style Baked Eggs with a sprinkle of wine in the recipe for a terrific continental touch.

Some of the greatest breakfast dishes are not those traditionally served in the A.M. But have you ever thought of serving hot deviled eggs for breakfast? These take a little more time so you'll want to prepare them on a leisurely morning. Or you can make them ahead of time, chill them, and heat them up just before serving. A blend of two delicious sauces gives my Hello Sunshine Deviled Eggs a rich, layered taste. And if you want an egg recipe that could win contests, treat yourself to my Curried Easter Eggs Extraordinaire. Named in honor of one of my favorite holidays, these spicy eggs are just right for a special festive meal. Bake a batch of my Sweet Perfection Cinnamon Rolls, and wrap them up in a basket for the perfect accompaniment.

At our house, we all take turns preparing our favorite breakfasts each morning. When Rick puts on his chef hat, he whips up sensational Port Charles French Toast made with thick, springy sourdough bread. When there's no sourdough bread around, you can get that sourdough taste by using buttermilk instead of milk in the recipe. He tops off the sliced French toast with dabs of sour cream and a slice of orange for garnish.

Amy is the pancake expert in our house. Her enthusiasm for pancakes is rivaled only by Aunt Jemima's. She sometimes surprises us with breakfast in bed and carries in a tray of her Pancake Clouds. You'll love these pancakes that are so light they almost rise off the plate. Try serving them with honey or applesauce instead of maple syrup. Being rather impulsive, Amy has also created a variation on a pancake theme—Amy's Pancake Sandwiches. You'll be hooked on this intriguing combination of bacon, pancakes and boiled eggs.

Now Blackie is a beginning cook. His first efforts at making breakfast went no further than opening a cereal box. So I taught him how to make my "Anyone Can" Omelet. This recipe is perfect for even the most inexperienced beginners.

Of course, there are those mornings when you're really late, but in the time it takes to find your car keys and put on your coat to leave the house you can be sipping my Orange on the Run. We all know how good oranges are for us. All that Vitamin C can really energize you each morning. And with just 1 chopped orange and 1 egg you can mix up a thick, creamy shake that starts you off on a healthy morning.

We love to have friends over for breakfast, but we hate to have to putter around the kitchen while our company just sits and waits. Two of the most delicious answers to our breakfast entertaining needs are my billowing Rise and Shine Cheese Soufflé and Webber's Corned Beef Creation with poached eggs. You can poach the eggs in advance and simply reheat them when the time comes, placing one on top of each serving of hash. Sometimes some of the nurses and doctors from General Hospital come to visit on Sundays, and I prepare a breakfast buffet. A classic cheese quiche works beautifully for these occasions, with its flaky crust and rich mixture of Parmesan, Swiss and Cheddar cheeses. I picked up this next breakfast idea at the Versailles Room, Curried Fruits Versailles, which I serve with my quiche. These sweet cubes of pineapples, bananas and papayas can be lifted with toothpicks from their serving dish for a juicy bite-size breakfast treat.

Sometimes I pick up the greatest new breakfast ideas when I visit my friends' houses. Breakfast at Tiffany's means Blueberry Blintzes. I can smell the fresh baked blueberry aroma before I even get to her front door. Tiffany was an actress so her breakfasts are always dramatic masterpieces. These golden crêpes simmering with tart blueberry sauce are a feast in themselves.

When Rick and I recently visited New York for a medical seminar, we noticed that on Sundays breakfast was being replaced by brunch. Every restaurant seemed to offer a brunch specialty and at noon the cafés opened their doors to some pretty discerning brunch goers. One of the most unusual brunch recipes we brought back was a Zucchini Brunch Casserole topped with crispy bread crumbs. I think you'll find it an unusual taste treat with lots of steamed-in vitamins. I serve slices of my Banana Bread Bounty with the salad. Sometimes I make up a few small loaves when I'm in a wild baking mood and freeze them so I can always have plenty of banana bread on hand. Use banana bread for your sandwiches too. Gives a nice lift to the lunch box blues.

I'm one of those people who loves banana bread or toast with homemade fruit jam. I used to watch my mom pick ripe juicy strawberries from our garden and boil them in lemon juice and fructose before storing them in jars in the refrigerator. I make my own strawberry jam now, and though it takes a little extra effort it's so much better than store-bought preserves. And these make unique birthday gifts. When was the last time you got a homemade present made with tender loving care?

Whenever there's a birthday in the house I start the day off celebrating with my Birthday Morning Cake that all the kids loved. When the kids were young I added a design of sliced apples to the top with the number of apple slices corresponding to the birthday year. I've also included a terrific cake the kids can make. If they can open a can of fruit cocktail and turn on the oven they'll be able to whip up my Zippity-do-da Cake. And this cake lasts! One cake can be sliced into anywhere from 9 to 16 servings. Serve it fresh or heat it up and enjoy it with mugs of steaming hot chocolate.

Our breakfast recipes have really made us look forward to each new morning. We hope you'll enjoy our breakfast and brunch recipes as much as we do. They're our special "Good Morning" greeting from our family to yours.

Lesley's Breakfasts and Brunches

EGGS LESLEY
EGGS BENEDICT

HOLLANDAISE SAUCE
4 egg yolks
1 cup of butter, melted
Juice of 1 small lemon
Salt

4 English muffins, split and toasted
Butter or corn-oil margarine
8 slices of Canadian bacon
8 eggs, soft poached

1. Make Hollandaise Sauce: Beat the egg yolks with an electric mixer until light and lemon-colored. Add the melted butter slowly, beating constantly, and then add the lemon juice and salt to taste. Do not cook the sauce but set it aside at room temperature in a warm place. (This can be stored without curdling and brought to room temperature before use.)
2. Butter the toasted muffins. Top each half with a slice of Canadian bacon, then with a poached egg. Cover with the sauce.

8 PORTIONS

BLACKIE'S "ANYONE CAN" OMELET
OMELET

1 egg, lightly beaten
1 tablespoon milk
Pinch of salt
Pinch of paprika
2 teaspoons butter or corn-oil margarine

1. Combine all ingredients except the butter or margarine and beat with a wire whisk or fork.
2. Melt the butter or margarine in a small skillet or omelet pan over low heat. Pour the egg mixture into the skillet and cook, lifting the edges with a spatula and tilting the pan from side to side to allow the uncooked portion to run to the bottom to cook.
3. When the bottom is cooked (the top still runny), fold one third of the omelet over toward the center. Rest the edge of the pan on a plate and quickly turn the pan upside down, so the omelet slides out on the plate, folded into thirds.

1 PORTION

Variation: *Cheese Omelet:* Add ¼ cup grated Cheddar cheese to the omelet before folding it.

EASY EGGS

6 slices of Cheddar cheese
6 eggs
2 cups dairy sour cream
¼ cup milk
¼ teaspoon Durkee salad seasoning
3 English muffins, cut into halves, toasted

1. Butter a baking dish, 7½ x 11¾ inches. Arrange the cheese slices over the bottom of the dish.
2. Break 1 egg over each cheese slice. Combine the sour cream and milk and spoon over the top of the eggs. Sprinkle with the seasoning.
3. Bake in a 350°F. oven for about 20 minutes.
4. Serve on the 6 toasted English muffin halves.
6 PORTIONS

UP AND AT 'EM POACHED EGGS
POACHED EGGS

Poached eggs may be made the day before and stored in the refrigerator. To serve, place the cold eggs in a large pan of water at room temperature and bring it slowly to a boil. Remove each egg with a slotted spoon and blot it with a paper towel before serving. Most restaurants poach their eggs in advance in order to keep up with the orders during rush hour.

1½ quarts water
1 tablespoon white vinegar
1 teaspoon freshly squeezed lemon juice
½ teaspoon salt
4 eggs

1. Combine the water, vinegar, lemon juice and salt in a pan and bring to a slow boil.
2. Break the eggs, one at a time, into a shallow dish, and slide 2 eggs into the water, one at a time. Reduce the heat and simmer for 2 to 3 minutes, depending upon how firm you want the yolks to be. Remove the eggs from the water with a slotted spoon and dip each egg into a bowl of warm water to rinse it. Place the egg on a paper towel to absorb the water. Repeat the process with the other 2 eggs.
4 PORTIONS

CURRIED EASTER EGGS EXTRAORDINAIRE
CURRIED EGGS

8 eggs, hard-cooked
2 cups milk, hot
2 tablespoons butter or corn-oil margarine
2½ tablespoons flour
⅛ teaspoon salt
Pinch of white pepper
1 teaspoon curry powder
¼ teaspoon ground ginger
¼ teaspoon Worcestershire sauce
1 teaspoon freshly squeezed lemon juice

1. Cut the eggs lengthwise into halves. Remove the yolks, being careful not to tear the whites.
2. Arrange the egg whites in a 9-inch glass pie pan or shallow baking dish.
3. Mash the egg yolks or rub them through a sieve to add later to the sauce.
4. Put the milk in a saucepan over low heat.
5. In another saucepan, melt the margarine and add the flour, stirring constantly. Cook the flour and margarine for 3 minutes. *Do not brown!*
6. Remove the flour and margarine from the heat and add the simmering milk all at once, stirring constantly with a wire whisk.

7. Put the sauce back over low heat and cook slowly for 20 minutes, stirring occasionally. When the sauce is cooked, remove from the heat, add all remaining ingredients, and mix well.
8. Add ½ cup of the sauce to the mashed egg yolks and mix well. Fill the 16 egg-white halves equally with the egg-yolk mixture. Pour the remaining sauce evenly over the tops of the eggs. Bake at 350°F. for 20 minutes, or until the eggs are lightly browned.

8 PORTIONS

HELLO SUNSHINE DEVILED EGGS
HOT DEVILED EGGS

This takes a little time, but it's worth it for a special occasion. The eggs can be made ahead and chilled, then put in a hot oven just before serving.

6 hard-cooked eggs
1 teaspoon prepared mustard
¼ cup Béchamel Sauce (recipe follows)
Pinch of salt
½ cup Mornay Sauce (recipe follows)
½ cup grated Parmesan or Romano cheese
Paprika

1. Cut the eggs lengthwise into halves. Remove the yolks to a bowl. Place the egg whites on an ovenproof serving dish and set aside.
2. Rub the yolks through a fine sieve. Add the mustard, béchamel sauce and salt and mix well. Fill the egg whites with the egg-yolk mixture.
3. Cover eggs with the Mornay sauce and sprinkle with grated cheese. Bake in a 425°F. oven for approximately 15 minutes. Sprinkle with paprika just before serving.

6 PORTIONS

BÉCHAMEL SAUCE

⅓ cup butter
½ medium-size onion, finely chopped
½ cup flour
3 cups hot milk
1 teaspoon salt
Pinch of white pepper
1 teaspoon dried parsley, crushed, using a mortar and pestle
Pinch of freshly grated nutmeg

1. Melt the butter in a saucepan. Add the onion and cook until soft.
2. Add the flour and cook for a few minutes longer, stirring constantly.
3. Add the milk and seasonings, stirring vigorously, and cook slowly, still stirring, until thickened.
4. Cook for about 25 minutes longer, until the sauce is thick and smooth, stirring occasionally.

3 CUPS SAUCE

MORNAY SAUCE

2 cups Béchamel Sauce (preceding recipe)
2 egg yolks
½ cup freshly grated Parmesan, Gruyère or Romano cheese
1 tablespoon butter

1. Heat the béchamel sauce and combine with the egg yolks, stirring constantly. Remove sauce from the heat as soon as it starts to boil.
2. Add the cheese and butter and stir until all is mixed thoroughly. (This sauce cannot be boiled or it will curdle and lose its good flavor.)

2½ CUPS SAUCE

SUPER SWISS-STYLE BAKED EGGS
SWISS-STYLE BAKED EGGS

2 teaspoons corn oil
2 eggs
¼ cup grated Swiss cheese
1 teaspoon sherry

1. Heat the corn oil in a small skillet.
2. Break the eggs into the skillet. When the whites are set, sprinkle with grated cheese.
3. Sprinkle (don't pour) the wine over them and cover. Cook until the yolks are set.

2 PORTIONS

TIFFANY'S BLUEBERRY BLINTZES
BLUEBERRY BLINTZES

8 Crêpes (see Index)
2 cups ricotta cheese
3 tablespoons sugar, or 2 tablespoons pure crystalline fructose
1 teaspoon vanilla extract
1 cup frozen blueberries, unthawed
BLUEBERRY SAUCE
1 cup frozen blueberries, thawed
¼ cup sugar or 3 tablespoons pure crystalline fructose
2 tablespoons water

1. Combine the ricotta cheese, sugar or fructose and vanilla extract in a food processor with a metal blade and blend until completely smooth.
2. Put the cheese mixture in a bowl. Add the cup of frozen blueberries and mix well.

3. Spoon some of the cheese mixture evenly down the center of each crêpe and fold the crêpe around the mixture. Place the crêpes, seam side down, in a flat baking dish and bake at 425°F. for 10 minutes, or until the tops are lightly browned.
4. Combine all sauce ingredients in a saucepan and slowly bring to a boil. Place half of the mixture in a blender container and blend until smooth. Return to the saucepan and combine with the half that contains the whole blueberries.
5. Place the crêpes on serving plates and spoon 2 tablespoons of the blueberry sauce over the top of each one.

4 OR 8 PORTIONS

PANCAKE CLOUDS
FLUFFY PANCAKES

4 eggs, separated
1 cup dairy sour cream
1 cup cottage cheese
1 tablespoon sugar
¾ teaspoon baking soda
½ teaspoon salt
¾ cup sifted flour

1. Beat the egg whites until stiff but not dry. Set aside. Beat the egg yolks until creamy.
2. Add the sour cream and cottage cheese to the egg yolks and blend thoroughly.
3. Add the sugar, baking soda and salt to the sifted flour and sift again. Add dry ingredients to the cottage cheese and egg mixture and mix thoroughly. Fold the egg whites in.
4. Cook on a heated buttered griddle or skillet, using approximately 2 tablespoons of batter per pancake (or less if you want smaller pancakes), until bubbles form on the top. Turn and brown the other side.
5. Serve with warm syrup, honey or applesauce.

4 TO 6 PORTIONS

AMY'S PANCAKE SANDWICHES
OLD-FASHIONED PANCAKE SANDWICHES

Four 3-inch Fluffy Pancakes (preceding recipe)
4 slices of bacon, cooked crisp
4 eggs
2 tablespoons butter or corn-oil margarine
¼ cup maple syrup

1. Prepare the pancakes and bacon and set aside in a warm place.
2. Break the eggs into gently boiling water and cook for 5 minutes or until the yolks are set the way you like them.
3. Spread 2 pancakes with butter or margarine and place on serving plates. Place 2 cooked eggs on each of them and place the bacon on top. Cover with the other 2 pancakes and butter the tops. Pour syrup over the top.

2 PORTIONS

PORT CHARLES FRENCH TOAST
SOURDOUGH FRENCH TOAST

3 eggs
½ cup buttermillk
¼ cup milk
4 slices of sourdough bread (or 8 slices of regular bread)
2 tablespoons butter or corn-oil margarine
Pure maple syrup
Sour cream

1. The night before you plan to serve this, combine the eggs, buttermilk and milk and beat well. Place the bread in a flat baking dish.

Pour the egg mixture over the bread, piercing each slice all over with the tines of a fork to allow the bread to absorb the egg mixture. Cover the dish and refrigerate overnight.
2. In the morning, heat the butter or corn-oil margarine in a large skillet. Place the bread in the skillet, pouring the remaining liquid over the bread in the skillet. Cook until bread slices are golden brown on both sides.
3. Remove from the skillet to a serving plate and serve with pure maple syrup and sour cream.

4 PORTIONS

Variation: If sourdough bread is not available, use ¾ cup buttermilk instead of ½ cup buttermilk and ¼ cup milk.

ZUCCHINI BRUNCH CASSEROLE
ZUCCHINI AND CHEESE CASSEROLE

1½ pounds zucchini
4 eggs, lightly beaten
½ cup milk
1 pound grated Monterey Jack or mozzarella cheese
1 teaspoon salt
2 teaspoons baking powder
3 tablespoons flour
½ cup bread crumbs
Corn-oil margarine

1. Preheat oven to 350°F. Wash the zucchini and cut into ½-inch slices. Place in a steamer basket over boiling water and steam for 3 minutes. Drain and cool.
2. Beat the eggs lightly and add the milk, grated cheese, salt, baking powder and flour. Add the zucchini and mix well.
3. Pour into a buttered 2-quart casserole dish and sprinkle the top with bread crumbs. Dot with margarine. Bake for 35 to 40 minutes.

6 TO 8 PORTIONS

RISE AND SHINE CHEESE SOUFFLÉ
CHEESE SOUFFLÉ

1 cup milk
2 tablespoons butter or corn-oil margarine
3 tablespoons flour
4 egg yolks
½ teaspoon salt
Pinch of cayenne
½ teaspoon Worcestershire sauce
¾ cup grated Cheddar cheese
5 egg whites, at room temperature
Pinch of salt
⅛ teaspoon cream of tartar

1. Preheat oven to 400°F. Place the milk in a saucepan over low heat and bring to a boil. Melt the butter or margarine in another larger saucepan and add the flour, stirring constantly for 3 minutes, being careful not to brown.
2. Remove the flour and butter mixture from the heat and add the boiling milk all at once, stirring with a wire whisk. Return the pan to the heat and allow the sauce to come to a boil, stirring constantly, for 1 minute. Again remove from the heat.
3. Add the egg yolks, one at a time, mixing thoroughly with a wire whisk. Add the salt, cayenne and Worcestershire sauce and mix well. (If you are entertaining and plan to serve this later, you may stop at this point and resume later.)
4. Cover and reheat to lukewarm before adding the beaten egg whites (or just proceed to finish the soufflé without interruption). Add the cheese and mix well.
5. Place the egg whites in a large mixing bowl with the salt and cream of tartar and beat un-til stiff but not dry. Add one quarter of the egg whites to the cheese sauce and stir in. Fold the remaining three quarters of the egg whites into the sauce. *Do not overmix!*
6. Spoon the batter into an 8-inch soufflé dish and set in the preheated oven. Reduce the heat immediately to 375°F. and cook for 20 to 25 minutes. Serve immediately.

6 PORTIONS

SLEEP LATE QUICHE
CHEESE QUICHE

Pastry for 9-inch, 1-crust pie
2 tablespoons butter or corn-oil margarine
¼ pound Swiss cheese, coarsely grated
¼ pound Cheddar cheese, coarsely grated
1 tablespoon grated Parmesan cheese
3 tablespoons flour
⅛ teaspoon grated nutmeg
4 eggs
2 cups light cream

1. Prepare the pastry and fit it into the quiche pan; set aside. Heat the butter in a small saucepan until dark brown and cool slightly. Keep warm.
2. Combine the Swiss, Cheddar and Parmesan cheeses with 1 tablespoon of the flour and the nutmeg and mix well. Pour into the pastry-lined pan.
3. Beat the eggs and 1 tablespoon of flour. Add the cream and the other tablespoon of flour and mix well. Force this mixture through a fine sieve, draining it over the cheese mixture in the pie plate. Add the melted butter over the top.
4. Set the quiche pan on a cookie sheet, and bake in a 375°F. oven for 30 minutes. Reduce the heat to 350°F., and bake for 15 to 20 minutes longer.

6 TO 8 PORTIONS

WEBBER'S CORNED BEEF CREATION
CORNED BEEF HASH

1 tablespoon butter or corn-oil margarine
1 small onion, finely chopped
1 tablespoon Worcestershire sauce
1 pound cooked or canned corned beef, diced
    (about 2 cups)
1 large baked potato with skin, diced
½ cup beef broth
¼ teaspoon freshly ground black pepper
4 poached eggs

1. Melt the butter or margarine in a skillet and sauté the onion over low heat until it is soft and clear.
2. Add all other ingredients except the poached eggs and mix well. Cook until the hash is thoroughly heated and all of the liquid is absorbed.
3. Serve topped with poached eggs.

4 PORTIONS

CHICKEN SALAD SENSATIONAL
CURRIED CHICKEN SALAD

3 large chicken breasts with skin, boned
Water
1 teaspoon salt
1 cup finely chopped celery
1 large onion, coarsely chopped
2 cups shelled walnuts, coarsely chopped
2 cups mayonnaise
1 teaspoon curry powder
Pinch of salt
Pinch of pepper

2 cans (8 ounces each) pineapple chunks, cut into
    halves
Lettuce leaves for salad plates, chilled

1. Place the chicken breasts in water to cover. Add the salt, celery and onion and bring to a boil. Reduce the heat and simmer until the chicken is fork-tender. Remove from the heat and cool to room temperature. Store in the cooking liquid in the refrigerator overnight.
2. Next morning, remove the chicken from the broth and remove the skin. Cut each chicken breast into ½-inch cubes.
3. Place the walnuts on a cookie sheet in the center of a 350°F. oven for 8 to 10 minutes, or until golden brown. Watch them carefully as they burn easily. Set aside.
4. Combine the mayonnaise, curry powder, salt and pepper, and mix well.
5. Toss the chicken, pineapple chunks and walnuts lightly together. Add the mayonnaise mixture and again toss lightly.
6. Place lettuce leaves on 8 chilled plates and divide the salad onto the plates.

8 PORTIONS

SO DELICIOUS TURKEY SALAD
TURKEY SALAD

2 heads of Boston lettuce
4 cups coarsely chopped cooked turkey meat
1 cup sliced water chestnuts, drained
1 pound seedless grapes, cut into halves
1 cup sliced celery
1½ cups mayonnaise
1½ teaspoons curry powder
1 tablespoon soy sauce
1 can (20 ounces) lychees, drained

(Recipe continues)

1. Tear the lettuce into bite-size pieces; rinse, and drain well. Set aside in the refrigerator.
2. Combine the turkey, water chestnuts, grapes and celery and mix thoroughly. Combine the mayonnaise, curry powder and soy sauce.
3. Combine the lettuce, turkey mixture and mayonnaise mixture. Reserve 1 cup of the lychees to place on top of the salads. Cut the others into quarters and add to the salad mixture; toss thoroughly.
4. Divide onto 6 chilled salad plates and place the reserved lychees on top.

6 PORTIONS

Variation: Use one 20-ounce can pineapple chunks, drained, in place of the lychees.

SUNRISE TOMATO SALAD
FRESH TOMATO SALAD

6 tomatoes, peeled and chopped
1 red onion, peeled and chopped
2 tablespoons sugar
2 teaspoons salt
4 cups shredded iceberg lettuce
4 slices of bacon
2 tablespoons cider vinegar

1. Combine the tomatoes, onion, sugar and salt in a bowl and let stand in the refrigerator for about 2 hours.
2. Place 1 cup shredded lettuce in each of 4 chilled soup plates and set aside.
3. Cook the bacon in a skillet until crisp. Remove and drain on a paper towel. Spoon the cider vinegar into the hot bacon fat and add the juice from the tomato and onion mixture. Place skillet over low heat while you divide the tomato-onion mixture over the lettuce in

the soup bowls. Then bring the sauce to a boil and pour some over the top of each serving.

4 PORTIONS

COOL AS A CUCUMBER SHRIMP BOATS
CUCUMBER SHRIMP BOATS

4 large cucumbers
½ pound cooked small shrimps
½ pound cooked crab meat, flaked
Lettuce leaves to line platter
Fancy Dressing (recipe follows)

1. Halve the cucumbers lengthwise and scoop out to form the boats.
2. Combine the seafood and stuff into the boats.
3. Arrange on a lettuce-lined platter and spoon ¼ cup of the dressing over each half cucumber. Serve chilled.

8 PORTIONS

FANCY DRESSING
LOUIS DRESSING

¾ cup mayonnaise
¼ cup chili sauce
2 tablespoons freshly squeezed lemon juice
¼ cup minced celery
½ cup dairy sour cream
2 tablespoons sweet pickle relish
½ teaspoon dillweed, crushed, using a mortar and pestle
¼ cup minced onion

1. Combine all ingredients and mix thoroughly. Chill and serve over Cucumber Shrimp Boats.

ABOUT 2 CUPS

SWEET PERFECTION CINNAMON ROLLS
CINNAMON ROLLS

1 cup warm milk
1 package active dry yeast (check the date on the package)
1 tablespoon vanilla extract
1½ cups sugar, or 1 cup pure crystalline fructose
¼ cup melted corn-oil margarine
2 eggs, lightly beaten
1 teaspoon salt
3½ cups unbleached white flour
Melted corn-oil margarine
1 tablespoon ground cinnamon

1. Pour the warm milk into a large warm mixing bowl and sprinkle the yeast over the top of it. Stir until the yeast is dissolved, about 5 minutes.
2. Add ¾ cup of the sugar or ½ cup fructose, ¼ cup melted margarine and lightly beaten eggs to the yeast and mix well.
3. Combine the salt and flour. Add 3 cups of the flour mixture, ½ cup at a time, to the sugar and eggs, mixing thoroughly. Turn dough onto a floured board and knead it, adding the remaining flour mixture until the dough is no longer sticky and is easy to handle, but still a soft dough. Roll out ½ inch thick to a 14-inch square. Brush with melted margarine.
4. Combine the cinnamon and remaining sugar or fructose and sprinkle generously over the dough.
5. Form into an even long roll. Chill.
6. Cut into slices approximately 1 inch wide and place the slices on a lightly oiled cookie sheet, arranging them on the pan so that the sides touch. Let rise in a warm place until doubled in volume, about 45 minutes. The oven of a gas stove or an electric oven with the light on provides the right warmth.
7. Preheat the oven to 375°F. Bake for 20 to 25 minutes.

ABOUT 14 ROLLS

Variation: *Pecan Rolls:* Add 1 cup finely chopped pecans after step 4, sprinkling them evenly over the cinnamon-sugar mixture just before forming the long roll.

BANANA BREAD BOUNTY
BANANA BREAD

½ cup milk
1 teaspoon cider vinegar
½ cup corn-oil margarine
1 cup sugar, or ⅔ cup pure crystalline fructose
2 eggs, lightly beaten
2 cups flour
Pinch of salt
1½ teaspoons baking soda
1 cup mashed bananas (3 medium)
½ cup chopped walnuts

1. Combine the milk and vinegar and set aside to sour.
2. Cream the margarine, sugar and eggs. Sift the flour, salt and baking soda together.
3. Add the dry ingredients to the creamed margarine mixture alternately with the soured milk and mashed bananas, and mix thoroughly. Stir in the chopped walnuts.
4. Pour into an oiled loaf pan 9 x 5 x 3 inches, and bake at 350°F. for 1½ hours. Cool on a rack.
5. Cut into thin slices and make small sandwiches with butter or cream cheese.

1 LOAF, 12 TO 16 SLICES

CURRIED FRUITS VERSAILLES
CURRIED FRUITS

Fresh fruits (pineapple, papayas, bananas, etc.)
    in bite-size cubes
Lemon juice
CURRY SAUCE
¾ cup white wine (Chablis is best)
¾ cup chicken broth
2 teaspoons curry powder
2 tablespoons cornstarch
3 tablespoons water
½ cup raisins
¾ cup grated coconut
½ cup toasted slivered almonds (optional)

1. Prepare the fruits in bite-size cubes and refrigerate, sprinkling with lemon juice to prevent discoloration.
2. Bring the wine, chicken broth and curry powder to a boil. Reduce the heat and simmer for 30 minutes. Stir the cornstarch and water together to form a slurry. Add to the chicken broth mixture and stir until thickened.
3. Add the raisins and coconut and mix well. At the last minute, add the sliced almonds if desired. Keep sauce warm in a chafing dish. Place toothpicks in the fruit cubes and arrange them on a serving dish beside the chafing dish.

2 CUPS SAUCE, ENOUGH FOR 6 TO 8 PORTIONS

BIRTHDAY MORNING CAKE
GINGERBREAD UPSIDE-DOWN COFFEE CAKE

⅓ cup butter
⅓ cup sugar or ¼ cup pure crystalline fructose
1 egg, beaten
¾ cup molasses
2 cups flour
2 teaspoons baking powder
½ teaspoon salt
¼ teaspoon baking soda
2 teaspoons ground cinnamon
1 teaspoon ground ginger
¾ cup buttermilk
FOR THE BOTTOM OF THE PAN
2 tablespoons butter
½ cup light corn syrup
½ cup chopped walnuts
2 medium-size apples, peeled and thinly sliced

1. Preheat oven to 350°F. Cream the butter and sugar. Add the beaten egg and mix thoroughly until smooth. Add the molasses and again mix well.
2. Combine all of the dry ingredients and add alternately with the buttermilk.
3. Prepare a 9-inch square cake pan: Melt 2 tablespoons butter in it. Add the corn syrup and nuts and spread evenly over the entire inner surface of the pan. Arrange the sliced apples artistically in the bottom of the pan.
4. Pour the batter into the pan. Bake in the preheated 350°F. oven for 1 hour.
5. Turn the cake out of the pan immediately after removing from the oven.

9 TO 16 SERVINGS, DEPENDING ON HOW YOU CUT IT

ZIPPITY-DO-DA CAKE
THROWN-TOGETHER CAKE

(when the children want to cook)

1 cup sugar
1 egg, lightly beaten
1½ cups flour
1 teaspoon baking soda
½ teaspoon salt
1 can (8 ounces) fruit cocktail with juice
1 teaspoon vanilla extract
¼ cup brown sugar
¼ cup chopped walnuts

1. Preheat oven to 350°F. Combine all ingredients except the brown sugar and walnuts in a bowl and mix thoroughly.
2. Pour into an oiled loaf pan 9 x 5 x 3 inches, and sprinkle the brown sugar and walnuts over the top. Bake for 35 to 40 minutes.

1 LOAF, 9 TO 16 SLICES

MOTHER'S STRAWBERRY JAM
STRAWBERRY JAM

2 pounds ripe strawberries
2 tablespoons freshly squeezed lemon juice
1½ cups pure crystalline fructose, or 2 cups sugar
5 tablespoons powdered pectin

1. Sort, wash, and hull the strawberries. Crush the berries, 1 cup at a time, with a potato masher.

2. Measure the strawberries before putting them in a saucepan to be sure you have 2 cups. If less than 2 cups, add enough water to make 2 cups.
3. Place over high heat, add the lemon juice and fructose, and bring the berries to a full rolling boil that cannot be stirred down.
4. Add the powdered pectin and bring to a full rolling boil again. Boil hard for 4 minutes.
5. Remove from the heat and skim with a metal spoon. Ladle into a hot, sterilized 16-ounce jar and seal. Store in the refrigerator after the jar reaches room temperature. (If you are increasing this recipe to make several jars, follow the procedures for canning and preserving provided by the manufacturer of the jars, which often involve paraffin, boiling water baths, wire racks, and so on.)

1 POUND JAM

ORANGE ON THE RUN
ORANGE SHAKE

(breakfast on the run)

1 orange, peeled and chopped
½ cup water
⅓ cup nonfat dry milk powder
1 teaspoon vanilla extract
1 egg, dipped into boiling water for 30 seconds before breaking
1½ teaspoons sugar, or 1 teaspoon pure crystalline fructose
¾ cup crushed ice

1. Combine all ingredients in a blender container and blend until completely smooth and of a creamy, thick consistency.

1 PORTION

Bobbie Spencer

People have always complimented me on what great energy I have. They tell me if I could just bottle it I'd make a fortune. Well, the secret of my success is simple: I eat the right foods. Good healthy meals put the glow in my cheeks and the shine in my hair. They help me feel better and look better. I know we'd all like to find the fountain of youth but the next best thing is eating foods that give you an energy boost.

When I first heard the term "health food" I thought it was just a lot of alfalfa sprouts and seaweed. But I've found that many of the foods I adore I don't have to give up at all. There's a healthy, nonfattening way to prepare everything from spaghetti to bread!

Just as you exercise to keep your body toned, you can prepare my Special Shape-Up Dishes to feel fit and keep down your weight. I've also included some healthful recipes for entertaining guests. Your friends will enjoy these delicious dishes and won't have to dread stepping on the scale later.

One of my slim-down specials that company raves over is my Bouillabaisse Spencer. I fell in love with this classic Marseilles bouillabaisse recipe at a French restaurant that Aunt Ruby took me to one evening. I adapted my recipe so that I wouldn't have to count calories. My secret is using chicken broth for a creamy, healthy base. It makes a special meal served steaming hot in shell-shaped bowls, with slices of fresh French bread.

I also happen to be crazy about spaghetti. But all that oil and white-flour spaghetti isn't good for you. So I created my Slenderiffic Seafood Spaghetti casserole. The trick to making this scrumptious supper is using whole-wheat pasta and low-fat milk in the recipe. This entrée is entirely fat free. When I want to save a little money I substitute water-packed tuna for shrimps.

Italian food is also my brother's favorite. Luke teased me at first when I started on my healthy foods campaign. But he's not laughing now. Luke is a loyal fan of my luscious pasta and vegetable Pasta Primavera Salad. Again, I use only whole-wheat pasta and my low-calorie Vim and Vigor Dressing on the salad. You may add diced tofu to the vegetables to add protein to this endless-energy salad.

Use my oil-free Vim and Vigor Dressing with my Fit as a Fiddle Sticks too. Simply take celery sticks and steam them for 5 minutes. Arrange them in a glass baking dish, pour on the Vim and Vigor Dressing, and sprinkle on pimientos and capers for flavoring. I always make up an extra batch of these tart and crunchy celery sticks to store in my refrigerator for those late-night munchies.

That's another reason why I love health foods: they take minimal time to prepare. Working as a nurse in General Hospital I don't have loads of leisure time to spend fussing in the kitchen. My Paragon of Chicken Tarragon takes only 40 minutes to make if you prepare the tarragon sauce ahead of time. Lightly brown your chicken and sprinkle chopped parsley over the top. Serve it with my nutritious Brown Rice Pilaf and baked tomatoes for the best gourmet health meal you've ever tasted.

Now, most of us have one thing in common: somewhere along the line, growing up, we had someone warn us to "eat your vegetables, they're good for you." Not only are vegetables a wonderful source of vitamins, they can be served in many different and creative ways, in all sorts of delightful combinations. My favorite vegetarian recipe is Full o' Pep Peppers—stuffed bell peppers with crunchy water chestnuts and lentils. Believe it or not, this recipe not only gives me energy, it saves me energy. Why? Because I never have to worry about lunch the next day. I just wrap up the peppers and eat them cold for lunch.

Most lunchtimes you'll find me enjoying my Fountain of Youth Fruit Dip, yogurt poured over my favorite fruits: melon wedges, pineapple slices, grapes, pear slices. I bring this sensational concoction to work in a Tupperware container and enjoy yogurt and fruit with a slice or two of Bobbie's Bran Bread.

Most people think being health-conscious means never having desserts again. Not true! When holidays roll around with their seasonal cookies and cakes, you won't find me leaving the table. I make a mean Mincemeat Mousse that is a low-calorie dream. The use of ricotta cheese in the recipe cuts down the calories. Serve this in sherbet glasses and garnish with a cinnamon stick for a real holiday occasion. At night when I crave dessert, I bake Bananas Bobbie, using date sugar instead of cane sugar. (You can find date sugar at most health-food stores.)

I also love to make my Heavenly Wholesome Waffles sweetened with fresh honey. Sometimes, after dinner, I'll pull out the old waffle iron and mix up a batch of these nutritional seven-grain waffles; it only takes 6 minutes.

Top waffles off with your favorite flavor of ice milk and you've got a dessert party. My recipe makes about 8 waffles, so invite a few friends over. The interns at General Hospital love this dessert.

Our favorite eating place in Port Charles is Kelly's Diner. It's the perfect place to meet friends and relax a bit after a long hard day. Rose is the best hostess. She serves her famous chili to my friends, but she makes sure she has her Feeling Good Vegetable Medley on the menu for me. This piled-high bowl of steamed vegetables in a rich chicken broth is a real find! Also, Rose always has a huge bowl of the most delicious salad of bell peppers, peas, tuna, celery and cheese in her refrigerator. I figured she must come to work at dawn to make up a jumbo salad of such variety before the first customers arrived. But Rose, being my most practical friend, simply invented her Overnight Wonder Salad. She layers all the ingredients in a bowl filled with lettuce and refrigerates overnight. (The peas can be put into the salad frozen, unthawed.) The next morning she garnishes the top with diced fresh tomatoes and she's all set to go!

While all around us our friends are swapping stories of the day's adventures, Rose and I swap salad recipes. The winner of last week's salad bowl contest was my Hot and Healthy Spinach Supreme. You haven't tasted spinach salad until you've sampled this hot dish seasoned with chervil and tarragon. You'll love it.

Every step you take towards a more toned body is worth the effort. I hope my recipes soon become a healthy habit for you. Taking vitamins and exercising are great, but keeping fit begins with a plate of nutritional food. Discover the secret energy sources in my shape-up recipes and enjoy a new, healthier you!

Bobbie's Special Shape-Up Dishes

BOUILLABAISSE SPENCER
BOUILLABAISSE

2 pounds white-fleshed fish, cut into serving
    pieces
Freshly squeezed lemon juice
Salt
4¼ cups chicken stock
2 cups thinly sliced onions
1 leek, white part only, chopped
1 teaspoon minced garlic
3 large tomatoes, peeled, seeded and diced
2 tablespoons chopped fresh parsley
1 celery rib, finely chopped
1 bay leaf
⅛ teaspoon ground fennel
⅛ teaspoon dried thyme, crushed, using a mortar
    and pestle
⅛ teaspoon saffron
Freshly ground black pepper

2 cups dry white wine, preferably Chablis
Crusty French bread

1. Rinse the fish in cold water and pat dry. Place in a glass dish and pour lemon juice on both sides. Salt both sides lightly. Cover and refrigerate until ready to cook it.
2. Heat ¼ cup of the chicken stock in a deep casserole or kettle. Add the onions and leek and cook for 5 minutes. Add the remaining vegetables and seasonings, with 1 teaspoon salt, and mix well. Cook for 5 more minutes.
3. Arrange the fish on top of the vegetables. Pour remaining chicken stock and the wine over the fish. Cover and bring to a boil. Cook for 8 to 10 minutes, or until the fish has turned white.
4. Divide the fish into bowls and pour broth and vegetables over each serving. Pass the crunchy French bread to your guests at the table.

6 TO 8 PORTIONS

TOMATO SOUP SLIM
FRESH TOMATO SOUP

2 tablespoons butter or corn-oil margarine
2 medium-size onions, thinly sliced
½ teaspoon dried thyme, crushed, using a
    mortar and pestle
½ teaspoon dried basil, crushed, using a mortar
    and pestle
½ teaspoon salt
¼ teaspoon freshly ground black pepper
6 large tomatoes, peeled, seeded, and chopped
4 tablespoons whole-wheat flour
3½ cups chicken broth
1 cup low-fat milk

1. Melt the butter or margarine in a heavy kettle
   and add the onions, thyme, basil, salt and
   pepper. Simmer over medium heat until the
   onions are soft.
2. Add the chopped tomatoes and simmer for
   about 10 minutes. Combine the flour with
   enough of the chicken broth to form a thin
   paste and stir into the mixture.
3. Add the rest of the broth and simmer for 5
   minutes, stirring constantly. Place in a
   blender or food processor and blend until
   smooth.
4. Return to the heat and add the milk and mix
   well. Heat to serving temperature. Do not
   boil.

6 PORTIONS

MEATBALL SOUP OPERA
ARMENIAN MEATBALL SOUP

¼ pound lean ground lamb
¼ cup uncooked rice
2 tablespoons minced onion
2 tablespoons chopped parsley
Ground nutmeg
½ teaspoon salt
4½ cups chicken broth
1 egg, beaten
1 tablespoon freshly squeezed lemon juice

1. Combine the lamb, rice, onion, parsley,
   sprinkling of ground nutmeg and the salt; mix
   well. Form into balls the size of large marbles
   and set aside.
2. Bring 4 cups of the chicken broth to a boil and
   drop the meatballs into it. Reduce the heat
   and simmer, covered, for 30 minutes. Turn
   off the heat.
3. Combine the beaten egg and lemon juice in a
   bowl. Heat remaining ½ cup of chicken broth
   and slowly add it to the egg, stirring constantly. Stir this mixture into the hot soup.
4. Divide the meatballs among 4 warmed soup
   plates. Pour the soup over the meatballs and
   serve immediately.

4 PORTIONS

PARAGON OF CHICKEN TARRAGON
CHICKEN TARRAGON

TARRAGON SAUCE
2 cups chicken stock
1½ teaspoons finely chopped onion
2 tablespoons sherry wine
¼ cup dry white wine (Chablis is best)
2 tablespoons cornstarch
2 tablespoons cold water
1½ teaspoons dried tarragon, crushed, using a
    mortar and pestle

2 whole chicken breasts, boned, skinned and
    halved
1 tablespoon corn-oil margarine
1 small garlic clove, minced
Salt
Freshly ground black pepper
¼ cup finely chopped parsley for garnish

1. Make the sauce: Heat the chicken stock in a saucepan. In another pan, combine the onion and wines over fairly high heat, boiling until liquid has been reduced by one third.
2. When reduced, add the chicken stock to the wine mixture and lower the heat to medium. Allow the mixture to come to a simmering boil.
3. Dissolve the cornstarch in the water and add to the sauce, mixing thoroughly with a wire whisk. Add the tarragon and mix well. Set the sauce aside.
4. Remove all visible fat from the chicken. Heat the margarine in a skillet and sauté the garlic for 3 to 5 minutes. Salt and pepper the chicken breasts and place in the skillet with the garlic. Brown chicken lightly on both sides.
5. Place the browned chicken breasts in a baking dish and pour the sauce over them. Bake, uncovered, in a 350°F. oven for 20 minutes.
6. Sprinkle chopped parsley over each serving.
4 PORTIONS

SLENDERIFFIC SEAFOOD SPAGHETTI
SEAFOOD SPAGHETTI

3 quarts water
Salt
¾ pound dry whole-wheat fettuccine
¾ cup chicken stock
1 leek, white part only, finely chopped
⅓ cup dry white wine
⅛ teaspoon cayenne pepper
1½ cups low-fat milk, scalded
1 teaspoon freshly squeezed lemon juice
1 pound cooked shrimps, or 2 cans (7 ounces
    each) water-packed tuna, drained and flaked
½ cup grated Parmesan cheese

1. Bring the water to a boil in a large pot and add 1 tablespoon salt. Add the fettuccine noodles and cook for 8 minutes. Drain, rinse with hot water, and drain again. Set aside.
2. Heat ¼ cup of the chicken stock in a large skillet. Add the leek, wine, remaining chicken stock and ½ teaspoon salt and bring to a boil. Reduce the heat and simmer, uncovered, until reduced by half.
3. Add the cayenne pepper and the milk, a little at a time, and continue to simmer until the sauce is smooth and reduced by one fourth. Remove from the heat, add the lemon juice and shrimps, and mix well.
4. Place half of the noodles in a 2-quart casserole and cover with half of the sauce. Top with the remaining noodles, then with remaining sauce. Bake at 400°F. for 10 to 15 minutes.
5. Sprinkle Parmesan cheese over each serving.
6 PORTIONS

VEGETABLE DELIGHT
HERBED VEGETABLES

3 cups assorted vegetables
¼ cup chicken stock
¼ teaspoon salt
1 teaspoon dried sweet basil, crushed, using a
    mortar and pestle
¼ cup finely chopped fresh parsley
¼ cup finely snipped chives or green onion tops

1. Steam the vegetables over rapidly boiling water for about 5 minutes. Run under cold water to preserve their color and texture. Drain and set aside. Include leftover vegetables from your refrigerator.
2. Heat the chicken stock in a large skillet. Add all ingredients except the vegetables and mix thoroughly over low heat.
3. Add the steamed vegetables and mix well. Heat just to serving temperature. *Do not overheat!*

4 PORTIONS

BROWN RICE PILAF

2 tablespoons butter or corn-oil margarine
¼ cup chopped onion
¼ cup chopped celery
1 cup uncooked brown rice
2½ cups chicken broth
¼ teaspoon salt
⅛ teaspoon freshly ground black pepper
1 bay leaf
3 tablespoons Parmesan cheese

1. Melt the butter or margarine in an ovenproof 4-cup casserole dish. Add the onion and celery and cook over low heat until the onion is soft.

2. Stir in the rice and cook for 2 or 3 minutes. Add the chicken broth, salt and pepper. Bring to a boil. Place the bay leaf on top. Cover and bake at 350°F. for 20 minutes. Add more chicken broth as needed.
3. Just before serving, remove the bay leaf and stir the Parmesan cheese through the rice.

6 PORTIONS

FEELING GOOD VEGETABLE MEDLEY
VEGETABLE MEDLEY AU GRATIN

¼ cup chicken stock
2 medium-size onions, minced
2 garlic cloves, minced
½ teaspoon dried thyme, crushed, using a
    mortar and pestle
1 bay leaf
6 medium-size tomatoes, peeled and diced
1 teaspoon salt
1 teaspoon dried orégano, crushed, using a
    mortar and pestle
1 teaspoon freshly ground black pepper
6 medium-size zucchini, diced
½ green bell pepper, seeded and diced
¼ cup grated Parmesan cheese
¼ teaspoon grated nutmeg
2 cups finely chopped uncooked spinach
1 cup minced fresh parsley
¼ cup snipped chives
1 tablespoon dried sweet basil, crushed, using a
    mortar and pestle
2 cups grated Monterey Jack cheese
Paprika

1. Heat the chicken stock. Add the onions, garlic, thyme and bay leaf and cook over low heat for 5 minutes.
2. Add the tomatoes, salt, orégano and black pepper and mix well. Cover and cook for 10

more minutes. Add the zucchini and bell pepper and cook, covered, for 12 to 15 more minutes.

3. Remove from the heat and add all other ingredients except the Jack cheese and paprika; mix well. Spoon into au gratin dishes and sprinkle ¼ cup of Jack cheese and a little paprika over each. Bake, uncovered, at 350°F. for 15 minutes.

8 PORTIONS

STUFFED SPUD SUPREME
STUFFED BAKED POTATO

2 baking potatoes, washed and pierced with the tines of a fork
1 medium-size onion, finely chopped
¼ cup chicken stock
½ cup cottage cheese
2 tablespoons grated Parmesan cheese
2 tablespoons snipped chives or green onion tops

1. Preheat oven to 400°F. Bake the potatoes for at least 1 hour, longer if necessary (some potatoes take longer to bake than others).
2. Cut a thin slice from the top of each potato and remove the pulp, being careful not to tear the shells. Mash the potato pulp and set aside in a covered bowl. Keep the shells warm.
3. Simmer the onion in the chicken stock until clear and tender. Add the mashed potato, cottage cheese and Parmesan cheese and mix well. Heat thoroughly.
4. Heap the potato mixture back into the warm shells and garnish with the chives or green onion tops. If these are prepared in advance and need to be reheated at 350°F. for 10 to 15 minutes, add the chives or green onion tops after the reheating.

2 PORTIONS

FULL O' PEP PEPPERS
STUFFED BELL PEPPERS

1 cup uncooked brown rice
½ cup uncooked lentils
1½ cups chicken stock
¼ teaspoon salt
½ teaspoon dried thyme, crushed, using a mortar and pestle
8 small bell peppers, tops removed and seeded
1 tablespoon corn-oil margarine
⅔ cup water chestnuts (8-ounce can), diced
¼ cup finely chopped fresh parsley
1 tablespoon minced garlic
1 cup finely chopped onion
1 celery rib without leaves, finely chopped
2 small carrots, finely chopped
2 cups mushrooms, finely chopped

1. Combine the brown rice, lentils, chicken stock, salt and thyme. Cook until the rice and lentils are done, about 45 minutes. Add more chicken stock if needed.
2. Prepare the bell peppers and set aside. Melt the margarine and sauté the water chestnuts, parsley, garlic and all of the vegetables until tender. Combine with the rice and lentil mixture to make stuffing.
3. Stuff the vegetable and grain mixture, ½ cup per pepper, into the peppers. Set peppers in a baking pan with ¼ inch of water in it.
4. Bake, covered, at 325°F. for 45 minutes. Remove the cover and bake for an additional 15 minutes, or until the tops are browned.

8 PORTIONS

SHAPE-UP CAESAR SALAD
CAESAR SALAD

1 cup corn oil
1 garlic clove, minced
4 slices of day-old bread, cut into ¼-inch cubes
2 tablespoons grated Parmesan cheese
2 heads of romaine lettuce
CAESAR DRESSING
1 garlic clove, peeled and quartered
1 cup less 2 tablespoons garlic oil prepared to
    cover the croutons
1 teaspoon salt
3 tablespoons red-wine vinegar
¼ teaspoon sugar
¼ cup water
¼ teaspoon freshly ground black pepper
2 tablespoons freshly squeezed lemon juice
1 teaspoon Worcestershire sauce
½ teaspoon Dijon-style mustard
1 small garlic clove, minced
¼ cup grated Parmesan cheese
1 can (2 ounces) anchovy fillets, drained
    (optional)

1. Combine the corn oil and garlic in a jar with a tight-fitting lid and let stand in the refrigerator overnight.
2. Place the bread cubes on a cookie sheet or a shallow baking dish and bake in a 300°F. oven for about 25 minutes, or until cubes are golden brown in color; stir at least twice so that the squares will brown evenly.
3. Place the croutons in a jar with a tight-fitting lid. Put 2 tablespoons of the garlic oil in the jar and shake vigorously. Add the Parmesan cheese to the jar and again shake vigorously until the croutons are coated with oil and Parmesan cheese. Set aside.

4. Several hours before you plan to serve the salad, wash and dry the lettuce thoroughly. Tear it into bite-size pieces and put in a large bowl lined with a cloth to absorb any remaining moisture. Store in the refrigerator.
5. Combine all of the dressing ingredients in a jar with a tight-fitting lid and shake vigorously. Store in the refrigerator.
6. When ready to serve, remove the cloth from under the lettuce and add the salad dressing. Toss the salad until every leaf glistens. Add the croutons and again toss thoroughly. Serve on chilled plates.
8 PORTIONS

HOT AND HEALTHY SPINACH SUPREME
SPINACH SALAD

6 packages (10 ounces each) frozen chopped
    spinach
¾ cup dairy sour cream
½ cup coarsely chopped celery
6 tablespoons grated onion
2 tablespoons vinegar
1 tablespoon finely chopped parsley
1 teaspoon salt
1 tablespoon dried tarragon, crushed, using a
    mortar and pestle
1 tablespoon dried chervil, crushed, using a
    mortar and pestle
Finely grated carrot for garnish (optional)

1. Cook the spinach according to package directions and drain well.
2. Add the sour cream, chopped celery, grated onion, vinegar, parsley, salt, tarragon and chervil and mix well.
3. A pretty garnish is finely grated carrot sprinkled over the top.
12 PORTIONS

FIT AS A FIDDLE STICKS
CELERY STICKS VINAIGRETTE

1 large bunch of celery, cut into sticks
1 cup Vim and Vigor Dressing (recipe follows)
8 large cold lettuce leaves
1 jar (4 ounces) pimientos, cut into strips
¼ cup capers

1. Steam the celery sticks over rapidly boiling water for 5 to 7 minutes. Remove from the steamer and run under cold water. Drain.
2. Place the celery sticks in a glass baking dish and pour the dressing over them. Refrigerate all day or overnight before serving.
3. Place the lettuce leaves on 8 chilled salad plates and arrange the celery sticks on them. Place the pimiento strips and capers over the top.

8 PORTIONS

VIM AND VIGOR DRESSING
LOW-CALORIE VINAIGRETTE

¼ teaspoon salt
¼ cup red-wine vinegar
1 teaspoon pure crystalline fructose
⅛ teaspoon freshly ground black pepper
¼ teaspoon garlic powder
1 teaspoon Worcestershire sauce
2 teaspoons Dijon-style mustard
2 teaspoons fresh lemon juice
2 teaspoons corn oil
½ cup water

1. Dissolve the salt in the vinegar. Add all remaining ingredients. Pour into a jar with a tight-fitting lid and shake vigorously. Store in the refrigerator.

ABOUT 1 CUP DRESSING

PASTA PRIMAVERA SALAD

HERB DRESSING
1 cup Vim and Vigor Dressing (see recipe)
1 teaspoon dried orégano, crushed, using a mortar and pestle
1 teaspoon dried tarragon, crushed, using a mortar and pestle
1 teaspoon dried basil, crushed, using a mortar and pestle

½ cup diced carrot
½ cup peas
1 cup small pieces of broccoli
1½ cups diced yellow squash
1½ cups diced zucchini
1 cup diced onion
3 cups cooked whole-wheat spaghetti (⅓ pound dry)
2 teaspoons cornstarch
1 cup chicken stock
¼ cup grated Romano cheese
1 small tomato, peeled and diced

1. Prepare the dressing and refrigerate it. Steam the vegetables until just crisp-tender and set aside.
2. Prepare the spaghetti according to package directions. While it is cooking, dissolve the cornstarch in a little of the chicken stock. Combine with the remaining chicken stock and bring to a boil. Reduce the heat and stir over low heat until the sauce is thickened.
3. Place the drained spaghetti in a large bowl. Add the Romano cheese to the chicken stock mixture and stir. Pour over the spaghetti and toss thoroughly. Add the steamed vegetables and mix well. Divide onto 4 serving plates and garnish with the diced tomato.

4 PORTIONS

ENERGY EGGS IN ASPIC
DEVILED EGGS IN ASPIC

4 hard-cooked eggs, peeled and cut into halves
¼ cup mayonnaise
½ teaspoon salt
½ teaspoon onion juice
¼ teaspoon ground rosemary
¼ teaspoon dry mustard
ASPIC
2 envelopes unflavored gelatin
¼ cup cool water
3 cups chicken broth
3 tablespoons freshly squeezed lemon juice
2 tablespoons white vinegar
1 teaspoon salt
1 teaspoon onion juice
¼ cup chopped fresh parsley

Lettuce leaves or salad greens

1. Remove the yolks from the egg halves and place in a bowl. Set the egg whites aside.
2. Combine the egg yolks, mayonnaise, salt, onion juice, rosemary and mustard and stir well. Spoon the mixture into the egg whites, smooth the tops, cover, and chill.
3. Soften the gelatin in the cool water. Combine the chicken broth, lemon juice, vinegar, salt and onion juice in a saucepan and bring just to a boil. Reduce the heat and add the softened gelatin. Stir until gelatin is completely dissolved.
4. Chill the aspic in a bowl in the refrigerator until syrupy. Then spoon about ¼ inch in the bottom of each of 8 custard cups or small molds (or a glass dish for cutting into squares). Arrange the deviled eggs (filled side down in molds or custard cups, filled side up in the glass dish). Fold the chopped parsley into the remaining aspic and spoon over the eggs.
5. Chill for several hours before turning out on lettuce leaves or other salad greens.

8 PORTIONS

PRESTO PESTO
PESTO

¼ cup pine nuts
1 cup fresh basil leaves, chopped
4 large garlic cloves
¼ teaspoon salt
½ cup olive oil
¼ cup grated Parmesan cheese

1. Combine all ingredients except the oil and cheese in a blender container and blend until a paste is formed.
2. Add half of the oil and cheese and blend. Then add the remaining half of each and continue to blend. Store in the refrigerator to use hot or cold on pasta.

ABOUT 1½ CUPS SAUCE

WHOLE-WHEAT BREAD AU NATURAL
WHOLE-WHEAT BREAD

1½ cups milk
2 packages active dry yeast (check dates on packages)
½ cup lukewarm water
2 cups whole-wheat flour
3 to 3¼ cups white flour
⅓ cup brown sugar
1 teaspoon salt
½ cup molasses
3 tablespoons shortening, melted and cooled

1. Scald the milk until a film appears on top; *do not cook*. Cool to room temperature.
2. Sprinkle the yeast in the lukewarm water and leave until it bubbles.
3. Pour the whole-wheat flour into a large bowl, add 2 cups of the white flour, and mix. Make a hole in the flour mixture and pour in the cooled milk. Add the yeast, sugar, salt, molasses and shortening and stir well.
4. Add as much of the remaining white flour as needed to give the dough the right consistency, i.e., not sticky; probably about 1½ cups more flour. Knead the dough as you add the flour, punching and folding. When the right consistency is reached, fold dough into a hump and moisten with oil. Place in a warm bowl and cover. Let rise in a warm place until doubled in bulk.
5. Punch down the dough and knead again. Let it rise again.
6. Divide into 4 oiled bread pans and let rise for the last time.
7. Bake at 425°F. for 45 to 60 minutes. Remove loaves from the pans and cool on a rack. Butter the tops to keep the crusts soft.

4 LOAVES

BOBBIE'S BRAN BREAD
BREAKFAST BRAN BREAD

1 cup raisins
1½ cups Bran Buds
2¾ cups buttermilk
4 teaspoons baking powder
1 teaspoon baking soda
½ teaspoon salt
1 cup brown sugar
3 cups flour
1 egg, beaten
1 tablespoon vanilla extract
1 tablespoon Grand Marnier (optional)

1. Combine the raisins, Bran Buds and buttermilk and allow to stand for 15 minutes.
2. Add all other ingredients. Mix thoroughly and allow to stand for another 20 minutes.
3. Butter and flour 2 standard loaf pans, 9 x 5 x 3 inches, and divide the dough equally between them.
4. Bake in a 350°F. oven for approximately 1 hour and 20 minutes.

2 LOAVES, EACH ABOUT 16 SLICES

HEAVENLY WHOLESOME WAFFLES
SEVEN-GRAIN WAFFLES

¾ cup 7-grain cereal
2 eggs, separated
½ cup corn oil
3 tablespoons honey
2 cups milk
2¾ cups whole-wheat flour
1 tablespoon baking powder
1 teaspoon salt

1. Soak the cereal overnight if possible, but for at least 2 hours. Use just enough water to dampen the cereal.
2. Combine the egg yolks, oil, honey and milk and mix thoroughly.
3. Combine the flour, baking powder and salt and mix well. Add the soaked 7-grain cereal and again mix well.
4. Add the liquid mixture to the flour mixture and stir lightly. Add additional milk if necessary to thin sufficiently to ladle.
5. Beat the egg whites and add to the waffle mixture before baking.
6. Preheat the waffle iron and pour the mixture, ½ cup at a time, onto the hot iron. Bake for approximately 6 minutes.

8 OR 9 WAFFLES

FOUNTAIN OF YOUTH FRUIT DIP
YOGURT FRUIT DIP

1 cup plain yogurt
1 cup dairy sour cream
2 tablespoons honey
¾ teaspoon ground ginger
½ teaspoon freshly squeezed lemon juice
Grated lemon rind for garnish

1. Combine all ingredients except the lemon rind in a bowl and blend until smooth. Cover and refrigerate for 1 hour or longer to chill thoroughly and blend the flavors. Sprinkle with grated lemon rind.
2. This is good with whole strawberries, pineapple chunks, tiny bunches of seedless grapes, melon wedges, and banana, apple and pear slices. To prevent discoloring, dip the banana, apple and pear slices into lemon juice before arranging on a platter. You may also use this as a salad dressing.

ABOUT 2 CUPS DIP

BANANAS BOBBIE
BAKED BANANAS

2 tablespoons butter or corn-oil margarine
2 tablespoons date sugar

1 teaspoon ground cinnamon
4 ripe bananas

1. Combine the butter, date sugar and cinnamon in a saucepan and heat slightly. Set aside.
2. Peel a 1-inch-wide strip down the length of each banana, leaving the peel attached at the end. Roll the strip into a curl and secure with a toothpick.
3. Place the bananas, exposed side up, in a buttered baking dish. Brush the date-sugar mixture over the exposed portion. Bake at 350°F. for 15 minutes.

4 PORTIONS

Note: Date sugar is ground dried dates. It is available in most health-food stores.

MINCEMEAT MOUSSE

1 box (9 ounces) mincemeat
2½ cups part-skim ricotta cheese
2 teaspoons vanilla extract
3 tablespoons brandy
Cinnamon sticks for garnish, optional

1. Combine all mousse ingredients in a food processor with a metal blade and blend until mixture has a smooth, creamy consistency (this takes quite a while).
2. Store, covered, in the refrigerator for several hours or overnight before serving. It is best made a day in advance. Serve in sherbet glasses garnished with cinnamon sticks.

8 PORTIONS

Robert Scorpio's Cooking Secrets from a Secret Agent

"TACO MEAT ME UNDER THE BRIDGE"
TACO MEAT

7-bone beef roast (4 to 5 pounds)
Water
1 package (2½ ounces) commercial taco
    seasoning
1 can (4 ounces) chilies, seeded and diced
¾ cup green taco sauce

1. Place the roast in a pan with water to cover and cook at 325°F. until it can be torn apart with a fork, for 3 to 4 hours.
2. Remove from the pan and cool slightly. While still warm, remove the bones and gristle and shred the meat into a bowl. This is best done with your hands.
3. Add the taco seasoning, chilies and sauce and mix with your hands as you would a meat loaf. Divide into the quantities you will need for individual tacos, tostadas, quesadillas, Mexican salads, Mexican eggs, omelet fillings, etc.
4. Freeze. Reheat when ready to use.

10 TO 12 PORTIONS

ORIENT EXPRESS MEATBALLS
CHINESE MEATBALLS

1 pound ground beef
¾ cup minced celery
¼ cup chopped almonds
1 garlic clove, minced
1 teaspoon salt
½ cup soft bread crumbs
1 tablespoon soy sauce
2 eggs, lightly beaten
Cornstarch to coat the meatballs
2 tablespoons corn oil
4 cups cooked rice
Sweet-and-Sour Sauce (recipe follows)

1. Combine the ground beef, celery, almonds, garlic, salt, bread crumbs, soy sauce and eggs, and mix well.
2. Form into small balls and roll in cornstarch to coat all surfaces.
3. Heat the corn oil in a skillet and add the meatballs. Cook until thoroughly browned. Serve over fluffy rice and top with Sweet and Sour Sauce.

4 PORTIONS

SWEET-AND-SOUR SAUCE

1 cup chicken broth
½ cup sugar
½ cup vinegar
½ cup pineapple juice
2 teaspoons soy sauce
3 tablespoons cornstarch
¾ cup chopped green pepper
¾ cup pineapple chunks

1. Combine the chicken broth, sugar, vinegar, pineapple juice and soy sauce. Add the cornstarch and cook, stirring, until thickened, for 3 to 4 minutes.
2. Add the green pepper and pineapple chunks. Simmer long enough to heat thoroughly.

3 CUPS SAUCE

DARING DOLMAS
STUFFED GRAPE LEAVES

1 jar (8 ounces) grape leaves (30 to 35 leaves)
FILLING
1 large onion, finely chopped
1 garlic clove, minced
¼ cup olive oil
¾ cup cooked rice
2 tablespoons finely chopped fresh parsley
1 teaspoon dillweed, crushed, using a mortar and pestle
¼ cup chopped pine nuts
¼ cup dried currants
1 cup finely ground cooked lamb (optional)
2 tablespoons olive oil
¼ cup freshly squeezed lemon juice
1 to 1½ cups water

Plain yogurt and lemon wedges

1. Drain the grape leaves and place in a large bowl. Separate the leaves, cover with boiling water, and let soak for 20 to 30 minutes. Place on paper towels to drain.
2. Combine the filling ingredients and mix well. Place 1 tablespoon of the mixture on the base of each grape leaf, vein side up, and fold the left and right sides of the leaf over. Then roll toward the tip of the leaf, loosely enough to allow for expansion of the rice. Place the remaining leaves, if there are any, on the bottom of a saucepan into which the stuffed rolls will fit snugly; this helps prevent sticking. Pack the rolls into the pan, seam side down. Sprinkle with the 2 tablespoons olive oil and the lemon juice and then add the water. Place an ovenproof dish over the top as a weight.
3. Cover and cook over low heat for 1 to 1½ hours, adding water if necessary.
4. Serve hot or cold with yogurt and lemon wedges. If served cold, the meat is often omitted.

8 TO 10 PORTIONS

SCORPIO'S SOUPE AU PISTOU
SOUPE AU PISTOU

2 quarts chicken broth
3 medium-size potatoes, peeled and cut into 1-inch pieces
½ pound fresh green beans, cut up
3 carrots, sliced
1 medium-size onion, chopped
1 tablespoon salt
¼ teaspoon freshly ground black pepper
½ pound zucchini, sliced
1 can (16 ounces) navy beans
PISTOU SAUCE
4 garlic cloves, mashed
1 can (6 ounces) tomato paste
1 tablespoon dried basil, crushed, using a mortar and pestle

½ cup grated Parmesan cheese
½ cup chopped fresh parsley
¼ cup olive oil

1. In a large kettle, combine the broth, potatoes, green beans, carrots, onion, salt and pepper. Bring to a boil and simmer, covered, for 1 hour.
2. Add the zucchini and beans and simmer for an additional hour.
3. While the soup is simmering, make the sauce. Combine all sauce ingredients except the olive oil. With an electric beater, gradually beat in the oil until the mixture resembles a thick sauce. Just before serving, stir the sauce into the hot soup. Serve with French bread.

8 TO 10 SERVINGS

Variation: Add a dollop of sour cream to each serving.

MYSTERIOUS MOUSSAKA
MOUSSAKA

3 medium-size eggplants
Salt
¼ cup olive oil
2 onions, finely chopped
2 pounds lean lamb, ground
2 garlic cloves, minced
2 tomatoes, peeled and chopped
4 cups shredded raw zucchini
¼ cup finely chopped fresh parsley
1 can (8 ounces) tomato sauce
½ cup dry red wine
1 teaspoon dried orégano, crushed, using a mortar and pestle
½ teaspoon ground allspice
¼ teaspoon grated mace
Freshly ground black pepper
½ cup grated Monterey Jack cheese
½ cup grated Parmesan cheese

CUSTARD TOPPING
2 tablespoons butter or corn-oil margarine
3 tablespoons flour
3 cups milk
3 eggs, lightly beaten
Nutmeg

Parsley sprigs for garnish

1. Peel the eggplants and cut into ½-inch slices. Place in a baking dish and sprinkle both sides with salt. Set aside for at least 1 hour. Drain and place slices on oiled baking sheets. Brush with olive oil. Bake at 350°F. for 15 minutes, or until slightly browned. Turn over, brush with more olive oil, and bake for 10 to 15 minutes longer.
2. Heat remaining olive oil in a large skillet and sauté the onions until browned. Add the lamb and cook, stirring, until browned. Add the garlic, tomatoes, zucchini, parsley, tomato sauce, wine and seasonings and mix well. Simmer for 15 to 20 minutes, or until the liquid is markedly reduced and the mixture is thick. Combine the cheeses.
3. Place a layer of the eggplant slices on the bottom of an oiled deep 3-quart baking dish or casserole. Cover with a layer of the meat mixture, followed with a layer of cheese. Continue with the layers until all ingredients are used, ending with eggplant slices on top.
4. Make the custard topping: Melt 2 tablespoons butter or margarine in a saucepan. Stir in the flour. Remove from the heat and add the milk, mixing well. Return to the heat and bring to a boil, stirring constantly, and simmer for 2 minutes. Remove from the heat. Add the eggs and nutmeg and mix well. Pour custard over the eggplant and meat in the casserole.
5. Bake the moussaka at 350°F. for 45 to 60 minutes, or until it is browned and bubbling. Cut into squares and serve. Garnish with parsley sprigs.

12 PORTIONS

Variation: Use ground lean beef instead of lamb.

SLEUTH'S SUKIYAKI
SUKIYAKI

It is fun to put cushions around a coffee table in the living room and bring the electric frying pan to the table for a real Japanese-style dinner party.

1 pound boneless lean beef, cut very thin across the grain
1 package (6¾ ounces) rice sticks, broken into 3-inch lengths, soaked in water for 20 minutes and drained
1 can (8 ounces) bamboo shoots, drained
2 tablespoons corn oil
6 green onions, cut into 2-inch pieces
1 onion, sliced vertically into ¼-inch slices
2 cups sliced fresh mushrooms
1 pound tofu (soybean curd), cut into ¾-inch cubes
1 cup bite-size pieces of watercress
2 cups shredded Chinese cabbage
½ cup soy sauce
4 tablespoons sugar
½ cup saki (rice wine)

1. Arrange the sliced beef and all vegetables, rice sticks and tofu attractively on a large platter in separate rows.
2. Heat a large skillet or electric frying pan. Add the oil, half of the meat, half of the soy sauce and half of the sugar and cook for 1 minute, stirring.
3. Push the meat to one side and add half of the vegetables, tofu and rice sticks. Add half of the saki and cook for about 4 minutes.
4. With chopsticks or long-handled forks, transfer the contents of the pan to individual plates and serve.
5. Repeat the process with the other half of the ingredients.
4 PORTIONS

SWEET-AND-SOUR PORK

2 pounds lean pork, cut into 2-inch squares
3 tablespoons corn oil
⅓ cup water
1 can (20 ounces) pineapple chunks
¼ cup brown sugar
2 tablespoons cornstarch
½ teaspoon salt
⅓ cup cider vinegar
1 tablespoon soy sauce
1 cup sliced fresh mushrooms
½ green pepper, thinly sliced
½ onion, thinly sliced
1 can (8 ounces) water chestnuts, sliced
Steamed rice if desired

1. Brown the meat in 2 tablespoons of the corn oil. Add the water and simmer, covered, for 1 hour.
2. Drain the pineapple chunks, reserving the juice. Combine the pineapple juice, brown sugar, cornstarch, salt, vinegar and soy sauce and cook until thickened.
3. Heat remaining tablespoon of corn oil and sauté the mushrooms, green pepper and onion until tender.
4. Combine all ingredients except the rice and mix well. Serve over steamed rice if desired.
6 TO 8 PORTIONS

THE CHINESE CABBAGE CAPER
CHINESE CABBAGE

3 heads of Chinese cabbage
3 tablespoons peanut or corn oil

3 green onions, shredded
½ cup chicken broth
1 tablespoon soy sauce
1 tablespoon sherry
1 tablespoon cornstarch
1 teaspoon salt

1. Trim the outer leaves and the cores from the cabbage and cut into fine julienne strips. Parboil the strips in boiling water for 3 minutes. Cool in cold water and drain well.
2. Heat the oil in a heavy saucepan. Add the green onions and cook until they are soft. Add the drained cabbage and cook the vegetables for about 4 minutes.
3. Combine the chicken broth, soy sauce, sherry, cornstarch and salt, and stir into the vegetables.
4. Cook over low heat, stirring constantly, for 2 or 3 minutes longer, or until the sauce is clear and slightly thickened.

6 TO 8 PORTIONS

YORKSHIRE PUDDING WITH SHERRIED CREAM SAUCE

YORKSHIRE PUDDING WITH CHICKEN AND SHERRIED CREAM SAUCE

3 whole chicken breasts, cut into halves
¼ cup all-purpose flour
1 teaspoon salt
½ teaspoon paprika
Pinch of pepper
2 tablespoons corn oil
YORKSHIRE PUDDING
4 eggs
2 cups milk
2 cups sifted all-purpose flour (sift before measuring)

½ teaspoon baking powder
1 teaspoon salt
1 teaspoon dried tarragon, crushed, using a mortar and pestle

SHERRIED CREAM SAUCE
2 cups milk
3 tablespoons corn-oil margarine
¼ cup minced onion
3 tablespoons all-purpose flour
¾ teaspoon salt
¼ cup sherry

1. Wash the chicken breast halves and pat dry. Combine the flour, salt, paprika and pepper in a plastic bag. Place the chicken, a few pieces at a time, in the bag and coat thoroughly with the flour mixture.
2. Heat the oil in a skillet and sauté the chicken, turning until well browned on both sides. Place in a baking dish 9 x 13 inches or in 6 ovenproof au gratin dishes.
3. Preheat oven to 425°F. Combine all of the pudding ingredients in a bowl and mix with an electric mixer until smooth. Pour ½ cup of the batter around each half chicken breast in each au gratin dish, or pour the entire mixture around the edges of the large baking dish. Bake for 25 to 30 minutes, or until the pudding is puffed up and golden brown.
4. While the pudding is baking, make the cream sauce. Scald the milk. Melt the margarine and add the onion. Cook until the onion is soft and clear.
5. Add the flour and cook, stirring constantly, for 3 minutes. Remove from the heat and add the milk, at the boiling point, to the flour mixture rapidly, stirring with a wire whisk until smooth. Add the salt and mix well. Return to the heat and cook, stirring constantly, until thickened.
6. Remove from the heat. Add the sherry and mix well. Pour approximately ⅓ cup over each serving.

6 PORTIONS

THE GREAT PAELLA ESCAPADE
PAELLA

8 clams in the shell
8 large shrimps in the shell
4 tablespoons olive oil
6 garlic cloves, minced
1 frying chicken, cut into small pieces
3 large onions, finely chopped
1 cup uncooked long-grain white rice
1½ cups chicken broth
½ cup dry white wine (Chablis is best)
1 teaspoon powdered saffron
½ teaspoon paprika
1 teaspoon salt
½ teaspoon freshly ground black pepper
1 cup raw green peas
2 large tomatoes, diced
¼ cup grated Parmesan cheese
1 jar (4 ounces) pimientos, julienne cut
8 lemon wedges

1. Scrub the clams with a stiff brush until they are very clean and set aside.
2. Shell the shrimps, leaving the tails attached. Using a small sharp knife, make a shallow slit down the back of each shrimp and lift out the vein. If it does not all come out in one piece, use the point of the knife to scrape out the remaining portions. Wash out the incision well with cold water. Set shrimps aside.
3. Heat 2 tablespoons of the olive oil in a large skillet and add the garlic. Add the chicken pieces and sauté until the chicken is cooked and golden brown on all sides. Set aside.
4. In a paella pan or skillet, heavy casserole or roasting pan at least 3 inches deep, heat the remaining 2 tablespoons of olive oil. Add the onions and rice and cook, stirring, until the onion is tender and the rice is lightly browned, about 15 minutes.
5. Preheat oven to 400°F. While the rice and onions are cooking, bring the chicken broth to a boil and add the wine.
6. Crush the saffron and paprika together, using a mortar and pestle, and add to the chicken-stock and wine mixture. Add the salt and pepper.
7. Add the stock mixture to the rice and onions, mixing thoroughly. Bring to a boil and arrange the browned chicken pieces on top of the rice.
8. Scatter the peas and tomatoes evenly over the top, then sprinkle with Parmesan cheese.
9. Arrange the clams and shrimps on top.
10. Set the pan on the floor of the oven and bake, uncovered, for 35 to 45 minutes, or until all of the liquid has been absorbed by the rice, the rice is tender, and the clams are open. At no point after the paella is put into the oven should it be stirred.
11. When the paella is done, remove it from the oven, cover loosely with a towel, and allow to rest for 5 minutes. Garnish with strips of pimiento and wedges of lemon and serve.

4 PORTIONS

ICE PRINCESS CURRY
SEAFOOD CURRY

¼ cup butter or corn-oil margarine
2 onions, finely chopped
6 tablespoons flour
1 tablespoon curry powder
1 teaspoon salt
1½ teaspoons sugar, or 1 teaspoon pure crystalline fructose
¼ teaspoon ground ginger
1 cup chicken stock, warm
2 cups milk, warm

2 pounds (4 cups) cooked shrimps, lobster, crab or scallops, or a combination of seafood
1 teaspoon freshly squeezed lemon juice

1. Melt the butter or corn-oil margarine in the top pan of a double boiler over boiling water.
2. Add the onions and cook until soft.
3. Combine the flour, curry powder, salt, sugar and ginger and add to the onion mixture. Cook, stirring constantly, for 2 minutes.
4. Add the chicken stock and continue stirring until thickened. Then slowly add the warm milk, stirring constantly.
5. Cook over boiling water, stirring frequently, until thickened.
6. Add the seafood and lemon juice and mix thoroughly.
7. Serve over rice with curry condiments in separate bowls.

Condiment suggestions: chutney, chopped hard-cooked eggs, raisins, peanuts, almonds, pineapple chunks, chopped crisp bacon, shredded coconut, grated orange peel, diced tomatoes.
6 PORTIONS

CUBAN BEAN CONSPIRACY
CUBAN BLACK BEANS

1 pound dried black beans
6 cups water
2 tablespoons butter or corn-oil margarine
½ pound pork sausage
1 large onion, coarsely chopped
2 slightly tart large apples, peeled and diced
2 garlic cloves, minced
2 teaspoons salt
¼ teaspoon freshly ground black pepper
1 teaspoon dry mustard
1 teaspoon chili powder
¼ cup brown sugar

1½ cups tomato juice
¼ cup dark rum
Sour cream
Chopped green onions

1. Wash the beans and soak in the water overnight. Leave beans in the soaking water, add the butter or margarine, and bring to a boil. Reduce the heat, cover, and simmer until tender, about 2 hours.
2. Flatten the sausage in a skillet and brown one side. Turn, breaking sausage into chunks. Add the beans and all other ingredients except the rum, sour cream and green onions. Mix well and bring to a boil.
3. Pour into a 2-quart casserole and bake at 325°F. for 2 hours. At 5 minutes before serving, add the rum. Top each serving with a dollop of sour cream and with green onions.
8 PORTIONS

NIGHTCAP RENDEZVOUS
SHERBET DESSERT

½ cup water
½ cup sugar, or 5 tablespoons pure crystalline fructose
½ cup rum
1 pineapple, peeled and cubed
3 bananas, diced
1 quart lemon sherbet
½ cup shredded coconut

1. Boil the water and sugar together for 5 minutes. Cool and add the rum.
2. Combine the pineapple and bananas in a bowl and pour the rum mixture over them. Place in the refrigerator for 3 to 4 hours.
3. Divide the sherbet into 8 dishes and cover with the fruit and syrup. Top each serving with a tablespoon of shredded coconut.
8 PORTIONS

BAKLAVA ADVENTURE
BAKLAVA

SYRUP

2 cups sugar, or 1½ cups pure crystalline
    fructose
2 cups water
½ cup honey
1 teaspoon freshly squeezed lemon juice
1 cinnamon stick

1 cup raw almonds, finely chopped
1 cup finely chopped walnuts
1 cup butter or corn-oil margarine, melted
1 pound phyllo (fillo) pastry, thawed according
    to package directions
2 teaspoons ground cinnamon
⅛ teaspoon ground cloves
¼ cup sugar, or 3 tablespoons pure crystalline
    fructose

1. Combine the syrup ingredients in a saucepan
    and heat until the mixture spins a thread when
    lifted on a spoon. Cool and refrigerate until
    very cold, removing the cinnamon stick.
2. Place the almonds and walnuts on a cookie
    sheet in the center of a 350°F. oven for 8 to 10
    minutes, or until golden brown. Watch them
    carefully as they burn easily. Set aside. Leave
    the oven on at 350°F.
3. Coat the inner surface of a baking pan, 9 x 13
    x 2 inches, with melted butter or margarine.
    Line the pan with half of the fillo sheets,
    brushing each one with melted butter or mar-
    garine and pressing each sheet well into the
    corners and on the sides, cutting to fit when
    necessary.
4. Combine the toasted nuts, cinnamon, cloves
    and sugar or fructose and spread evenly over
    the fillo sheets. Top the nut mixture with the

remaining fillo sheets, brushing each one with
butter. Press the sheets firmly together at the
edges of the pan and trim with a sharp knife.
5. Brush the top of the baklava with melted but-
    ter or margarine. Using a very sharp knife,
    make ½-inch-deep cuts in diamond shapes.
    Bake at 350°F. for 30 minutes, then reduce the
    heat to 300°F. and bake for 30 minutes more,
    or until the top is golden brown.
6. Pour the cold syrup over the hot baklava
    when it comes from the oven, deepening the
    diamond-shaped cuts so the syrup can seep
    down between the layers.
7. After the baklava has cooled, cut the scored
    diamond-shaped pieces completely through
    with a sharp knife and separate for serving.

12 OR MORE PORTIONS

Variation: You may start with 5 or 6 fillo leaves
topped with several tablespoons of the filling,
then more fillo leaves, more mixture, and repeat
until the ingredients are used, with fillo leaves on
top.

RAIDERS OF THE RUM PUNCH
RUM PUNCH

1 pint dark rum
1 can (6 ounces) frozen lime juice
1 can (6 ounces) frozen orange juice
4½ cups water to dilute the frozen juices
1 can (6 ounces) frozen lemon juice, unthawed
2 cans (46 ounces each) pineapple juice
2 ounces Curaçao liqueur
1 pint Sauterne wine

1. Combine all ingredients and mix thoroughly.
    Serve in a punch bowl.

45 PORTIONS, 4 OUNCES EACH

Short Takes from General Hospital

Luke Spencer

LUKE'S CRAZY MIXED-UP STEW
BEEF STEW

1 pound stewing beef, cut into 1-inch cubes
½ cup flour
¼ cup butter or corn-oil margarine
½ pound fresh mushrooms, sliced (2 cups)
2 leeks, white part only, sliced
2 parsley sprigs
1 bay leaf
1 teaspoon salt
½ teaspoon freshly ground black pepper
½ teaspoon dillweed, crushed, using a mortar
   and pestle
½ teaspoon dried thyme, crushed, using a
   mortar and pestle
½ teaspoon dried savory, crushed, using a
   mortar and pestle
2 garlic cloves, pressed

½ cup water
1 bottle red wine (1 fifth)
2 carrots, scraped and cut into 1-inch rounds
1 turnip, diced
1 potato, peeled and diced
10 boiling onions, whole, peeled
1 package (10 ounces) frozen peas, thawed

1. Place the stewing beef in a plastic bag with the flour and shake until coated.
2. Heat the butter or margarine in a skillet. Sauté the mushrooms and leeks; remove vegetables from the skillet. Place the beef in the skillet and brown rapidly.
3. Return the mushrooms and leeks to the skillet with the beef and add the parsley, bay leaf, salt, pepper, dillweed, thyme, savory, garlic, water and half of the wine. Simmer for 30 minutes.
4. Add more of the wine and all vegetables except the peas; simmer for 1 additional hour. Remove the bay leaf and parsley. Add the peas and remaining wine and cook over medium heat for an additional 10 minutes.

4 PORTIONS

Rose Kelly

KELLY'S DINER CHILI
CHILI

1 pound dried pinto beans
Water
½ cup butter or corn-oil margarine
6 green onions, finely chopped
1 can (7 ounces) green chilies, seeded and
    chopped
2 garlic cloves, minced
3 pounds chopped sirloin
1 pound sausage meat
1 can (16 ounces) baked beans
1 can (4 ounces) pimientos
3 cans (28 ounces each) tomatoes
1 celery rib without leaves, chopped
½ pound fresh mushrooms, chopped (2 cups)
½ cup chopped green bell pepper
1 can (9 ounces) pitted ripe olives, chopped
½ cup chopped fresh parsley
1 bottle (12 ounces) chili sauce
2 teaspoons salt
1 teaspoon garlic salt
2 teaspoons freshly ground black pepper
1 tablespoon dried orégano, crushed, using a
    mortar and pestle
2 to 4 tablespoons chili powder, depending upon
    your taste buds
Sour cream (optional)
Snipped chives or green onion tops (optional)

1. Wash and drain the pinto beans. Soak in water to cover overnight. In the morning, bring
   to a boil in the soaking water. Reduce the heat
   and simmer for 2 to 3 hours, or until the beans
   are tender. Drain.
2. Melt the butter or margarine in a large skillet
   and add the onions, chilies and garlic and

sauté until onions are soft. Add the chopped
sirloin and cook over medium heat until
brown.
3. In another pan, brown the sausage and drain.
   Add to the onion-meat mixture and mix well.
   Transfer the entire mixture to an 8-quart kettle and add the beans, pimientos, tomatoes,
   celery, mushrooms, green pepper, olives,
   parsley and chili sauce. Mix well and bring to
   a boil. Reduce the heat and simmer for about
   30 minutes, stirring occasionally.
4. Stir in the seasonings, adding the chili powder
   a little at a time to taste as you go. Simmer for
   1¼ hours longer, stirring occasionally.
5. A dollop of sour cream and some snipped
   chives or green onion tops may be added on
   each serving.

12 TO 16 PORTIONS

Rose Kelly

ROSE'S OVERNIGHT WONDER SALAD
OVERNIGHT SALAD

1 head of iceberg lettuce, torn into bite-size
    pieces
1 small bell pepper, seeded and diced
1 medium-size red onion, finely chopped
½ cup chopped celery
3 packages (10 ounces each) frozen peas,
    unthawed
1 cup mayonnaise
2 tablespoons sugar, or 1½ tablespoons pure
    crystalline fructose
1½ cups grated sharp Cheddar cheese
8 slices of bacon, cooked crisp, drained and
    crumbled (½ cup crumbled bacon)
2 cans (7 ounces each) white tuna, chilled and
    drained
3 large tomatoes, peeled and diced, for garnish

1. Layer the ingredients in a large bowl, starting with the lettuce, then the green pepper, onion and celery. Sprinkle the frozen peas evenly over the top.
2. Combine the mayonnaise and sugar or fructose and spread evenly over the top. Sprinkle the grated cheese over the mayonnaise and then sprinkle the crumbled bacon over the cheese. Cover tightly and refrigerate overnight.
3. To serve, uncover the salad. Add the chilled, drained tuna and mix thoroughly. Serve the salad in large chilled salad bowls or plates and sprinkle the diced tomatoes over the top for color.

8 PORTIONS

FLOATING RIB FLANK STEAK
MARINATED FLANK STEAK

HONEY-SOY MARINADE
¼ cup soy sauce
3 tablespoons honey
2 tablespoons vinegar
1½ teaspoons garlic powder
1½ teaspoons ground ginger
¾ cup corn oil
1 green onion, finely chopped

2 to 3 pounds flank steak

1. Combine the marinade ingredients and mix well. Pour into a glass baking dish.
2. Place the flank steak in the marinade and marinate in the refrigerator overnight, turning over at least once.
3. Remove beef from the marinade and barbecue over hot coals to taste. Cut into desired serving sizes, following the grain of the meat.

6 TO 8 PORTIONS

Heather Webber

HEATHER'S HOT TAMALES
HOT TAMALE PIE

2 tablespoons corn oil
1 pound ground beef
2 large onions, chopped
1 large green bell pepper, chopped
1 garlic clove
3 tablespoons chili powder (2 tablespoons if you prefer milder flavor)
2 cups tomato sauce
1 cup water
½ teaspoon salt
Dash of Tabasco (optional)
1 cup corn muffin mix
1 cup cream-style corn
1 egg
Milk, enough to make a medium batter
½ cup grated Cheddar cheese
½ cup corn chips, crushed

1. Heat the corn oil in a skillet. Add the ground beef, onions and green pepper and brown, stirring occasionally.
2. Add the garlic, chili powder, tomato sauce, water, salt and Tabasco, and simmer for 35 minutes. Pour into a flat baking dish, 11¾ x 7½ inches.
3. Combine the muffin mix, corn, egg and milk and pour over the top of the mixture in the baking dish. Bake at 350°F. for 45 minutes.
4. Just before removing from the oven, sprinkle the cheese and corn chips over the top and brown.

6 PORTIONS

Index